TRYING
CONCLUSIONS

TRYING CONCLUSIONS

New and Selected Poems, 1961–1991

HOWARD NEMEROV

THE UNIVERSITY OF CHICAGO PRESS • CHICAGO & LONDON

Howard Nemerov, one of the twentieth century's most popular and critically ac-
claimed poets, was Poet Laureate of the United States from 1988 to 1990. In his
distinguished career he was awarded the Bollingen Prize for Poetry, the Theodore
Roethke Poetry Prize, a Guggenheim fellowship, and the first Aiken Taylor Award
for Modern American Poetry. *The Collected Poems of Howard Nemerov,* published
by the University of Chicago Press, won the National Book Award and the
Pulitzer Prize in 1978. At the time of his death in 1991, Mr. Nemerov was the
Mallinckrodt Professor Emeritus at Washington University in St. Louis.

The University of Chicago Press, Chicago 60637
The University of Chicago Press, Ltd., London
© 1991 by The University of Chicago
All rights reserved. Published 1991
Printed in the United States of America

00 99 98 97 96 95 94 93 92 91   5 4 3 2 1

ISBN (cloth): 0–226–57263–3

Library of Congress Cataloging-in-Publication Data
Nemerov, Howard.
    Trying conclusions: New and selected poems, 1961–1991 / Howard
Nemerov.
      p.   cm.
   I. Title.
PS3527.E5T79   1991
811′.54—dc20   91–3217
                                                    CIP

TO

NANCY GALBRAITH

AND

JENNIFER RUTLAND,

WITH LOVE

Contents

from GNOMES AND OCCASIONS *(1973)*

from THE WESTERN APPROACHES *(1975)*

from SENTENCES *(1980)*

from INSIDE THE ONION *(1984)*

from WAR STORIES *(1987)*

TRYING CONCLUSIONS *(1987–91)*

from

THE NEXT ROOM OF THE DREAM

(1962)

To Clio, Muse of History

On learning that The Etruscan Warrior
in the Metropolitan Museum of Art
is proved a modern forgery

One more casualty,
One more screen memory penetrated at last
To be destroyed in the endless anamnesis
Always progressing, never arriving at a cure.
My childhood in the glare of that giant form
Corrupts with history, for I too fought in the War.

He, great male beauty
That stood for the sexual thrust of power,
His target eyes inviting the universal victim
To fatal seduction, the crested and greaved
Survivor long after shield and sword are dust,
Has now become another lie about our life.

Smash the idol, of course.
Bury the pieces deep as the interest of truth
Requires. And you may in time compose the future
Smoothly without him, though it is too late
To disinfect the past of his huge effigy
By any further imposition of your hands.

But tell us no more
Enchantments, Clio. History has given
And taken away; murders become memories,
And memories become the beautiful obligations:
As with a dream interpreted by one still sleeping,
The interpretation is only the next room of the dream.

For I remember how
We children stared, learning from him
Unspeakable things about war that weren't in the books;
And how the museum store offered for sale
His photographic reproductions in full color
With the ancient genitals blacked out.

SANTA CLAUS

Somewhere on his travels the strange Child
Picked up with this overstuffed confidence man,
Affection's inverted thief, who climbs at night
Down chimneys, into dreams, with this world's goods.
Bringing all the benevolence of money,
He teaches the innocent to want, thus keeps
Our fat world rolling. His prescribed costume,
White flannel beard, red belly of cotton waste,
Conceals the thinness of essential hunger,
An appetite that feeds on satisfaction;
Or, pregnant with possessions, he brings forth
Vanity and the void. His name itself
Is corrupted, and even Saint Nicholas, in his turn,
Gives off a faint and reminiscent stench,
The merest soupçon, of brimstone and the pit.

Now, at the season when the Child is born
To suffer for the world, suffer the world,
His bloated Other, jovial satellite
And sycophant, makes his appearance also
In a glitter of goodies, in a rock candy glare.
Played at the better stores by bums, for money,
This annual savior of the economy
Speaks in the parables of the dollar sign:
Suffer the little children to come to Him.

At Easter, he's anonymous again,
Just one of the crowd lunching on Calvary.

TO THE MANNEQUINS

Adorable images,
Plaster of Paris
Lilies of the field,
You are not alive, therefore
Pathos will be out of place.

But I have learned
A fact about your fate,
And it is this:

After you go out of fashion
Beneath your many fashions,
Or when your elbows and knees
Have been bruised powdery white,
So that you are no good to anybody—

They will take away your gowns,
Your sables and bathing suits,
Leaving exposed before all men
Your inaccessible bellies
And pointless nubilities.

Movers will come by night
And load you into trucks
And take you away to the Camps,
Where soldiers, or the State Police,
Will use you as targets
For small-arms practice,

Leading me to inquire,
Since pathos is out of place,
What it is that they are practicing.

THE IRON CHARACTERS

The iron characters, keepers of the public confidence,
The sponsors, fund-raisers, and members of the board,
Who naturally assume their seats among the governors,
Who place their names behind the issue of bonds
And are consulted in the formation of cabinets,
The catastrophes of war, depression, and natural disaster:
They represent us in responsibilities many and great.
It is no wonder, then, if in a moment of crisis,
Before the microphones, under the lights, on a great occasion,
One of them will break down in hysterical weeping
Or fall in an epileptic seizure, or if one day
We read in the papers of one's having been found
Naked and drunk in a basement with three high school boys,
Of one who jumped from the window of his hospital room.
For are they not as ourselves in these things also?
Let the orphan, the pauper, the thief, the derelict drunk,
And all those of no fixed address, shed tears of rejoicing
For the broken minds of the strong, the torn flesh of the just.

DON JUAN TO THE STATUE

Dominant marble, neither will I yield!
The soul endures at one with its election,
Lover to bed or soldier to the field,
Your daughter's the cause of this & that erection.

ONE FOREVER ALIEN

When I become the land, when they will build
Blast furnaces over me, and lay black asphalt
For hundreds of miles across my ribs, and wheels
Begin to bounce interminably on the bone;
When I enter, at last, America, when I am
Part of her progress and a true patriot,
And the schoolchildren sing of my sacrifice,
Remembering the burial day of my birth—
Then even the efficient will have to forgive me,
The investigators approve my security,
And those that harden their hearts welcome me home.

Then, in that day, my countrymen,
When I shall come among you fleeced as the lamb
And in the diaper of the grave newly arrayed,
The Adam Qadmon, the greenhorn immigrant,
Shall pass the customs at the port of entry
Where the Guardian Lady lifts her flaming sword.
Forgiven the original sin of his origin,
He comes as a bond redeemed, as newly negotiable,
    To be as a soybean before you.

A SPELL BEFORE WINTER

After the red leaf and the gold have gone,
Brought down by the wind, then by hammering rain
Bruised and discolored, when October's flame
Goes blue to guttering in the cusp, this land
Sinks deeper into silence, darker into shade.
There is a knowledge in the look of things,
The old hills hunch before the north wind blows.

Now I can see certain simplicities
In the darkening rust and tarnish of the time,
And say over the certain simplicities,
The running water and the standing stone,
The yellow haze of the willow and the black
Smoke of the elm, the silver, silent light
Where suddenly, readying toward nightfall,
The sumac's candelabrum darkly flames.
And I speak to you now with the land's voice,
It is the cold, wild land that says to you
A knowledge glimmers in the sleep of things:
The old hills hunch before the north wind blows.

HUMAN THINGS

When the sun gets low, in winter,
The lapstreaked side of a red barn
Can put so flat a stop to its light
You'd think everything was finished.

Each dent, fray, scratch, or splinter,
Any gray weathering where the paint
Has scaled off, is a healed scar
Grown harder with the wounds of light.

Only a tree's trembling shadow
Crosses that ruined composure; even
Nail holes look deep enough to swallow
Whatever light has left to give.

And after sundown, when the wall
Slowly surrenders its color, the rest
Remains, its high, obstinate
Hulk more shadowy than the night.

IDEA

Idea blazes in darkness, a lonely star.
The witching hour is not twelve, but one.
Pure thought, in principle, some say, is near
Madness, but the independent mind thinks on,
Breathing and burning, abstract as the air.

Supposing all this were a game of chess.
One learned to do without the pieces first,
And then the board; and finally, I guess,
Without the game. The lightship gone adrift,
Endangering others with its own distress.

O holy light! All other stars are gone,
The shapeless constellations sag and fall
Till navigation fails, though ships go on
This merry, mad adventure as before
Their single-minded masters meant to drown.

SOMEWHERE

A girl this evening regrets her surrender with tears,
A schoolboy knows he will be unprepared tomorrow.
A father, aware of having behaved viciously,
Is unable to speak; his child weeps obstinately.
Somewhere a glutton waits for himself to vomit,
An unfaithful wife resists the temptation to die.

The stones of the city have been here for centuries,
The tides have been washing backwards and forwards
In sunlight, in starlight, since before the beginning.
Down in the swamp a red fox runs quietly, quietly
Under the owl's observation, those yellow eyes
That eat through the darkness. Hear the shrew cry!

Somewhere a story is told, someone is singing
Of careless love in the hands of its creditors.
It is of Yseult, Antigone, Tarquin with Lucrece,
The Brides in the Bath. . . . Those who listen
Lean forward bemused, rapt with the sweet seductions
Punishable by death, with the song's word: long ago.

De Anima

Now it is night, now in the brilliant room
A girl stands at the window looking out,
But sees, in the darkness of the frame,
Only her own image.

And there is a young man across the street
Who looks at the girl and into the brilliant room.
They might be in love, might be about to meet,
If this were a romance.

In looking at herself, she tries to look
Beyond herself, and half become another,
Admiring and resenting, maybe dreaming
Her lover might see her so.

The other, the stranger standing in cold and dark,
Looks at the young girl in her crystalline room.
He sees clearly, and hopelessly desires,
A life that is not his.

Given the blindness of her self-possession,
The luminous vision revealed to his despair,
We look to both sides of the glass at once
And see no future in it.

These pure divisions hurt us in some realm
Of parable beyond belief, beyond
The temporal mind. Why is it sorrowful?
Why do we want them together?

Is it the spirit, ransacking through the earth
After its image, its being, its begetting?
The spirit sorrows, for what lovers bring
Into the world is death,

The most exclusive romance, after all,
The sort that lords and ladies listen to
With selfish tears, when she draws down the shade,
When he has turned away,

When the blind embryo with his bow of bees,
His candied arrows tipped with flower heads,
Turns from them too, for mercy or for grief
Refusing to be, refusing to die.

BLUE SUBURBAN

Out in the elegy country, summer evenings,
It used to be always six o'clock, or seven,
Where the fountain of the willow always wept
Over the lawn, where the shadows crept longer
But came no closer, where the talk was brilliant,
The laughter friendly, where they all were young
And taken by the darkness in surprise
That night should come and the small lights go on
In the lonely house down in the elegy country,
Where the bitter things were said and the drunken friend
Steadied themselves away in their courses
For industrious ruin or casual disaster
Under a handful of pale, permanent stars.

THESE WORDS ALSO

There is her mother's letter on the table
Where it was opened and read and put down
In a morning remaining what it never was,
Remaining what it will not be again.

These words also, earth, the sun brings forth
In the moment of his unbearable brilliancy:
"After a night of drink and too much talk,
After the casual companions had gone home,
She did this. . . ." How the silence must have grown
Austere, as the unanswerable phone
Rang in a room that wanted to be empty.

The garden holds its sunlight heavy and still
As if in a gold frame around the flowers
That nod and never change, the picture-book
Flowers of somebody's forbidden childhood,
Pale lemony lilies, pansies with brilliant scowls
Pretending to be children. Only they live,
And it is beautiful enough, to live,
Having to do with hunger and reflection,
A matter of thresholds, of thoughtless balancings.

The black and gold morning goes on, and
What is a girl's life? There on the path
Red ants are pulling a shiny beetle along
Through the toy kingdom where nobody thinks.

VERMEER

Taking what is, and seeing it as it is,
Pretending to no heroic stances or gestures,
Keeping it simple; being in love with light
And the marvelous things that light is able to do,
How beautiful! a modesty which is
Seductive extremely, the care for daily things.

At one for once with sunlight falling through
A leaded window, the holy mathematic
Plays out the cat's cradle of relation
Endlessly; even the inexorable
Domesticates itself and becomes charm.

If I could say to you, and make it stick,
A girl in a red hat, a woman in blue
Reading a letter, a lady weighing gold . . .
If I could say this to you so you saw,
And knew, and agreed that this was how it was
In a lost city across the sea of years,
I think we should be for one moment happy
In the great reckoning of those little rooms
Where the weight of life has been lifted and made light,
Or standing invisible on the shore opposed,
Watching the water in the foreground dream
Reflectively, taking a view of Delft
As it was, under a wide and darkening sky.

THE END OF SUMMER SCHOOL

At dawn today the spider's web was cold
With dew heavy as silver to the sight,
Where, kicked and spun, with clear wings befouled,
Lay in the shrouds some victims of the night.

This morning, too, as if they had decided,
A few first leaves came loose and drifted down
Still slopes of air; in silence they paraded
Their ominous detachment to the lawn.

How strange and slow the many apples ripened
And suddenly were red beneath the bough.
A master of our school has said this happened
"Quiet as grass can ruminate a cow."

And now the seeds go on their voyages,
Drifting, gliding, spinning in quiet storms
Obedient to the air's lightest laws;
And where they fall, a few will find their forms.

And baby spiders, on their shining threads,
The middle air make glisten gold all day;
Sailing, as if the sun had blessed their roads,
Hundreds of miles, and sometimes out to sea.

This is the end of summer school, the change
Behind the green wall and the steady weather:
Something that turns upon a hidden hinge
Brings down the dead leaf and live seed together,

And of the strength that slowly warps the stars
To strange harbors, the learned pupil knows
How adamant the anvil, fierce the hearth
Where imperceptible summer turns the rose.

To David, about His Education

The world is full of mostly invisible things,
And there is no way but putting the mind's eye,
Or its nose, in a book, to find them out,
Things like the square root of Everest
Or how many times Byron goes into Texas,
Or whether the law of the excluded middle
Applies west of the Rockies. For these
And the like reasons, you have to go to school
And study books and listen to what you are told,
And sometimes try to remember. Though I don't know
What you will do with the mean annual rainfall
On Plato's Republic, or the calorie content
Of the Diet of Worms, such things are said to be
Good for you, and you will have to learn them
In order to become one of the grown-ups
Who sees invisible things neither steadily nor whole,
But keeps gravely the grand confusion of the world
Under his hat, which is where it belongs,
And teaches small children to do this in their turn.

GNOMES

A SACRIFICED AUTHOR

Father, he cried, after the critics' chewing,
Forgive them, for they know not what I'm doing.

LOVE

A sandwich and a beer might cure these ills
If only Boys and Girls were Bars and Grills.

MINIM

The red butterflies are so beautiful!
But they will not stand still to be looked at.

DEBATE WITH THE RABBI

You've lost your religion, the Rabbi said.
    It wasn't much to keep, said I.
You should affirm the spirit, said he,
And the communal solidarity.
    I don't feel so solid, I said.

We are the people of the Book, the Rabbi said.
    Not of the phone book, said I.
Ours is a great tradition, said he,
And a wonderful history.
    But history's over, I said.

We Jews are creative people, the Rabbi said.
    Make something, then, said I.
In science and in art, said he,
Violinists and physicists have we.
    Fiddle and physic indeed, I said.

Stubborn and stiff-necked man! the Rabbi cried.
    The pain you give me, said I.
Instead of bowing down, said he,
You go on in your obstinacy.
    We Jews are that way, I replied.

On the Threshold of His Greatness, the Poet Comes Down with a Sore Throat

> *Enthusiasm is not the state of a writer's soul.*
> —Valéry.[1]

For years I explored the pharmacopoeia
After a new vision. I lay upon nails
While memorizing the Seven Least Nostalgias.[2]
And I lived naked in a filthy cave,
Sneering at skiers, all one awful winter;
Then condescended, and appeared in tails
At the Waldorf-Astoria,[3] where I excelled
In the dancing of the Dialecticians' Waltz
Before admiring matrons and their patrons.

Those days, I burned with a hard, gemlike phlegm,
And went up like Excelsior[4] in a huff
Of seven-veiled symbols and colored vowels.
Flying from the alone to the Alone,[5]
My name appeared on every manifest
O.
    Everything, Bhikkhus, was on fire.[6]
Things are so different now. My reformation,
Glittering o'er my fault.[7] . . . Anyhow,

1. "Variety," tr. by Malcolm Cowley, in "An Introduction to the Method of Leonardo da Vinci."
2. Ancient druidical chants of immense length. Also referred to, in some early writers, as "The Small End of the Egg of Wisdom."
3. An hotel in New York City.
4. A poem by Henry Wadsworth Longfellow.
5. Plotinus, in Stephen Mackenna's translation.
6. In the present tense in Buddha's Fire Sermon addressed to a thousand monks at Gaya Head in Magadha. See Henry Clarke Warren, "Buddhism in Translations" (Harvard, 1922), Ch. IV, Sec. 73. See also William Empson, "Poems" (London, 1935), and T. S. Eliot, "The Waste Land" (1922), Part III, "The Fire Sermon," ad fin. Bhikkhus = monks, or priests.
7. Shakespeare, "Henry IV Part One," 1.2.236.

It's very quiet here at Monsalvat.[8]
The kids are singing in the cupola,[9]
But quietly. The good old psychopomp
Who comes to give my shots is terribly kind:
Procurasin at night in massive doses,
Repentisol next morning when I wake.
An unpretentious life, with late quartets
Among the early frescoes, a few friars
Asleep in their coffins[10] off to one side,
Angels adoring[11] where the jet planes wailed.
Evenings, we all eat from the same Grail.

Gin a body meet a body[12]
Under the boo[13]
    Under the bo
        Under the bodhi tree
—*All is illusion,*[14] *all is vanity*[15]—
    Nobodhi there but me and me[16]

Metaphysics at mealtime gets in my hair.[17]

8. The Grail Castle. Richard Wagner, "Parsifal," "Lohengrin." See also Nemerov, "The Melodramatists" (1949), pp. 155 & ff.

9. T. S. Eliot, "The Waste Land," line 202: "Et O ces voix d'enfants, chantant dans la coupole!" Mr. Eliot's note attributes the line to Verlaine, "Parsifal," but probably the sentiment, in one form or another, goes back to antiquity. Cf. Kafka, "The Castle," where K., telephoning for permission to enter the Castle, hears in the receiver "the hum of countless children's voices—but yet not a hum, the echo rather of voices singing at an infinite distance."

10. See James Joyce's celebrated story "The Dead," in *Dubliners*.

11. Painting by Fra Angelico in the National Gallery, London.

12. Note the increased profundity of the Burns song in the new context.

13. Cf. T. S. Eliot, "Fragment of an Agon": "Under the bam / Under the boo / Under the bamboo tree."

14. The Buddha.

15. Ecclesiastes. The collocation of these two representatives of Eastern and Western tradition, here at the collapse of the poem, may not be an accident.

16. The Buddha achieved illumination and Buddahood under the bo tree from the perception that all the forces of evil threatening him arose from within himself.

17. Wallace Stevens, "Les Plus Belles Pages": "Theology after breakfast sticks to the eye."

Notes by Cyril Limpkin, M.A. (Oxon.), Fellow in American literature at the University of Land's End, England.

Note on Notes. These notes have not the intention of offering a complete elucidation of the poem. Naturally, interpretations will differ from one reader to another, and even, perhaps, from one minute to the next. But because Modern Poetry is generally agreed to be a matter of the Intellect, and not the Feelings; because it is meant to be studied, and not merely read; and because it is valued, in the classroom, to the precise degree of its difficulty, poet and critic have agreed that these Notes will not merely adorn the Poem, but possibly supersede it altogether.

LION & HONEYCOMB

He didn't want to do it with skill,
He'd had enough of skill. If he never saw
Another villanelle, it would be too soon;
And the same went for sonnets. If it had been
Hard work learning to rime, it would be much
Harder learning not to. The time came
He had to ask himself, what did he want?
What did he want when he began
That idiot fiddling with the sounds of things?

He asked himself, poor moron, because he had
Nobody else to ask. The others went right on
Talking about form, talking about myth
And the (so help us) need for a modern idiom;
The verseballs among them kept counting syllables.

So there he was, this forty-year old teenager
Dreaming preposterous mergers and divisions
Of vowels like water, consonants like rock
(While everybody kept discussing values
And the need for values), for words that would
Enter the silence and be there as a light.
So much coffee and so many cigarettes
Gone down the drain, gone up in smoke,
Just for the sake of getting something right
Once in a while, something that could stand
On its own flat feet to keep out windy time
And the worm, something that might simply be,
Not as the monument in the smoky rain
Grimly endures, but that would be
Only a moment's inviolable presence,
The moment before disaster, before the storm,
In its peculiar silence, an integer
Fixed in the middle of the fall of things,
Perfected and casual as to a child's eye
Soap bubbles are, and skipping stones.

from

THE BLUE
SWALLOWS

(1967)

LANDSCAPE WITH FIGURES

What a dream of a landscape!
Cries Mrs. Persepolis, and I
Agree, my gaze follows hers
Out to the giant recumbent
Hills in their sullen haze
Brooding some brutal thought
As it were about myself &
Mrs. Persepolis, who are now
Alone in a closed garden
With various flowers and bees
And a feeble fountain that drips
On a stone in a heart-shaped
Pool with a single leopard-
Like toad immobilized all
Morning at his predatory
Meditation, making me think
Mrs. Persepolis not too old
With her bright voice and
Wrinkling skin at the wrist
Patterned in sunburnt diamonds
But still a game old girl
(And I a game old guy) good
For a tumble in the August
Grass right at the center
Of the dream of a landscape

Till I see her glittering eye
Has taken this thought exactly
As the toad's tongue takes a fly
So that we laugh and the moment
Passes but Mrs. Persepolis
As the bees go about their business
And we go in to have lunch
(How cold the house, the sudden
Shade! I shiver, and Mrs.
Persepolis shivers too, till
Her bangles bangle) my dear
Mrs. Persepolis, beautiful
Exile from childhood, girl
In your rough and wrinkled
Sack suit, couldn't you cry
Over that funny moment when
We almost fell together
Into the green sleep of the
Landscape, the hooded hills
That dream us up & down?

A LIFE

Innocence?
In a sense.
In no sense!

Was that *it?*
Was *that* it?
Was that it?

That was it.

THE HUMAN CONDITION

In this motel where I was told to wait,
The television screen is stood before
The picture window. Nothing could be more
Use to a man than knowing where he's at,
And I don't know, but pace the day in doubt
Between my looking in and looking out.

Through snow, along the snowy road, cars pass
Going both ways, and pass behind the screen
Where heads of heroes sometimes can be seen
And sometimes cars, that speed across the glass.
Once I saw world and thought exactly meet,
But only in a picture by Magritte.

A picture of a picture, by Magritte,
Wherein a landscape on an easel stands
Before a window opening on a land
scape, and the pair of them a perfect fit,
Silent and mad. You know right off, the room
Before that scene was always an empty room.

And that is now the room in which I stand
Waiting, or walk, and sometimes try to sleep.
The day falls into darkness while I keep
The TV going; headlights blaze behind
Its legendary traffic, love and hate,
In this motel where I was told to wait.

The Companions

There used to be gods in everything, and now they've gone.
A small one I remember, in a green-gray stone,
Would watch me go by with his still eyes of a toad,
And in the branch of an elm that hung across the road
Another was; he creaked at me on windless days.
Now that he's gone I think he might have wanted praise
For trying to speak my language and getting that far at least
Along on the imitation of a speaking beast.

Maybe he wanted help, maybe they all cried out
As they could, or stared helpless to enter into thought
With "read me," "answer me," "teach me how to be
Whatever I am, and in return for teaching me
I'll tell you what I was in you, how greater far
Than I are seeking you in fountain, sun, and star."
That's but interpretation, the deep folly of man
To think that things can squeak at him more than things can.
And yet there came those voices up out of the ground
And got into my head, until articulate sound
Might speak them to themselves. We went a certain way
Together on that road, and then I turned away.

I must have done, I guess, to have grown so abstract
That all the lonely summer night's become but fact,
That when the cricket signals I no longer listen,
Nor read the glowworms' constellations when they glisten.

Sarajevo

In the summer, when the Archduke dies
Past the year's height, after the burning wheel
Steadies and plunges down the mountainside,
The days' succession fails from one to one
Still great as kings, whose shock troops in the field
Begin to burnish their green shoots to gold.

That undeclared war always takes the field
In the summer, when the Archduke dies,
And the blind spills buried beneath the wheel
Are risen, spears bespoken through earth's side
To sacrifice their fast and turning gold
In ransom for the blood of all in one.

Now that blood will be redeemed for gold
Eagle and crown aglitter in the wheel,
In the summer, when the Archduke dies,
Europe divides and fuses, side and side,
Ranging the human filings on the field
Of force, held by the magnet, not yet one.

Still empty of its food the battlefield
Waits on the harvest and the great wain's wheel,
The vessels wait at hearth and harborside.
In the summer, when the Archduke dies,
Fate and the fortune of the game are one,
The green time turns to a heavy red, to gold.

And now responsible men on either side
Acknowledge their allegiance to the One
God of battles whose name is writ in gold,
The same whose coin, that cruelly blazing wheel,
In the summer, when the Archduke dies,
Buys earth as though it were a peasant's field.

The wildly streaming past now falls to one
Plunge on the oldest number of the wheel,
The zero twice redeemed in suicide,
Last blood sport of the green civilian field
Where the old world's sun went down in gold
In the summer when the Archduke died.

To a Scholar in the Stacks

When you began your story all its words
Had long been written down, its elements
Already so cohered in such exact
Equations that there should have seemed to be
No place to go, no entrance to the maze.
A heart less bold would have refused to start,
A mind less ignorant would have stayed home.

For Pasiphaë already had conceived
And borne her bully boy, and Daedalus
Responding had designed the darkness in
Its mystical divisions; Theseus,
Before you came, descended and returned,
By means of the thread, many and many a time.
What was there that had not been always done?

And still, when you began, only because
You did begin, the way opened before you.
The pictured walls made room, received your life;
Pasiphaë frowned, the Sea King greeted you,
And sighing Ariadne gave the thread
As always; in that celebrated scene
You were alone in being alone and new.

And now? You have gone down, you have gone in,
You have become incredibly rich and wise
From wandering underground. And yet you weary
And disbelieve, daring the Minotaur
Who answers in the echoes of your voice,
Holding the thread that has no other end,
Speaking her name whom you abandoned long ago.

Then out of this what revelation comes?
Sometimes in darkness and in deep despair
You will remember, Theseus, that you were
The Minotaur, the Labyrinth and the thread
Yourself; even you were that ingener
That fled the maze and flew—so long ago—
Over the sunlit sea to Sicily.

SUNDAY

He rested on the seventh day, and so
The chauffeur had the morning off, the maid
Slept late, and cook went out to morning mass.
So by and large there was nothing to do
Among the ashtrays in the living room
But breathe the greyish air left over from
Last night, and go down on your knees to read
The horrible funnies flattened on the floor.

It's still a day to conjure with, if not
Against, the blessed seventh, when we get
A chance to feel whatever He must feel,
Looking us over, seeing that we are good.
The odds are six to one He's gone away;
It's why there's so much praying on this day.

AT THE AIRPORT

Through the gate, where nowhere and night begin,
A hundred suddenly appear and lose
Themselves in the hot and crowded waiting room.
A hundred other herd up toward the gate,

Patiently waiting that the way be opened
To nowhere and night, while a voice recites
The intermittent litany of numbers
And the holy names of distant destinations.

None going out can be certain of getting there.
None getting there can be certain of being loved
Enough. But they are sealed in the silver tube
And lifted up to be fed and cosseted,
While their upholstered cell of warmth and light
Shatters the darkness, neither here nor there.

To the Governor & Legislature of Massachusetts

When I took a job teaching in Massachusetts
I didn't know and no one told me that I'd have to sign
An oath of loyalty to the Commonwealth of Massachusetts.
Now that I'm hooked, though, with a house
And a mortgage on the house, the road ahead
Is clear: I sign. But I want you gentlemen to know
That till today it never once occurred to me
To overthrow the Commonwealth of Massachusetts
By violence or subversion, or by preaching either.
But now I'm not so sure. It makes a fellow think,
Can such things be? Can such things be in the very crib
Of our liberties, and East of the Hudson, at that?
So if the day come that I should shove the Berkshire Hills
Over the border and annex them to Vermont,
Or snap Cape Cod off at the elbow and scatter
Hyannis to Provincetown beyond the twelve-mile limit,
Proclaiming apocalypsopetls to my pupils
And with state troopers dripping from my fingertips
Squeaking "You promised, you broke your promise!"
You gentlemen just sit there with my signature
And keep on lawyer-talking like nothing had happened,
Lest I root out that wagon tongue on Bunker Hill
And fungo your Golden Dome right into Fenway Park
Like any red-celled American boy ought to done
Long ago in the first place, just to keep in practice.

A Full Professor

Surely there was, at first, some love of letters
To get him started on the routine climb
That brought him to this eminence in time?
But now he has become one of his betters.

He has survived, and even fattened on,
The dissertation and the discipline.
The eyes are spectacled, the hair is thin,
He is a dangerous committeeman.

An organism highly specialized,
He diets on, for daily bill of fare,
The blood of Keats, the mind of poor John Clare;
Within his range, he cannot be surprised.

Publish or perish! What a frightful chance!
It troubled him through all his early days.
But now he has the system beat both ways;
He publishes and perishes at once.

A Relation of Art and Life

Into the sacred precincts come the savage sages,
The shamans meager of body, furious of mind
From lonesome meditations near to madness,
The wizards, wardens of the kindless wonders,
And prophets, who seek to bring catastrophe
Under a copyright, and doom to its publication.
With eyeballs able to swivel in their sockets,
These are the universal joints between the All and Nothing;
Driven by dreams to the interpreters of dreams,
They are without sin, and casting their first stones.
Out of the desert they come, and from the mountains,
From contemplation of those still sterilities
Or the repetition of the ocean tides deriving
Each one his remedy for men, his unpriced pearl
To sell to the priesthood to be a secret saying
To say over sacrifices, to be cast in contempt
Before popular swine. The secret sayings are such
As destroy societies; to have one is to hold
A hot coal in the mouth, and what mouth would stay closed?
The sages have arrived; they are breathing fire.

First, Sexual Licence, all sweat and dishevel
And a scrotum stuffed like the sack of Santa Claus;
Then Drunken Disorder, big with his liquid bulk
Of unzipped incompetence and vomit and sleep.
And now comes Salutary Hatred, self-beshitten;
And Anarchy that acts, with Apathy his twin
That lets be acted; and Narcosis in his kinds,
That works the doorway to the double dream
Where pose the caterpillar and the butterfly
Their contradictions to the sunshine or the shroud.
The priesthood serenely appraises the secrets
And grades them according to order and harmony,
Establishing values, deriving from every vision
Its proper doctrine: from drunkenness a jail,
From sexual license the institution of wedlock,
From anarchy and apathy the armed services,
Industrial development from drugged sleep,
And from hatred the holy mystery of the law;
Absorbing outrage into probability,
Improving virtue from the average of vice.

Now avant-garde movies are made, money is given
For receiving the sages and making them at home
In the accursed culture; with subversive civility
The bride-price is paid that the City be saved.
And the dreams of the desert are digested in art.
To reactionary mirages now the sages retire
In their neoclassical Cadillacs, miraculous
Ranches arise on the sands, and roses red and white
Bloom in the dust at the door; the sages get busy
Revising their visions comformably with fact.

While in the sacred precincts now the scribes
Already expound the Word that was without the world
An idiot star, a shining in chaos and underived,
That now is marketable cosmos, and a cause
To be fought for and against, to be taught in schools
With grades, degrees, and fellowships, and gowns,
And hides, and hoods, by master ham and doctor clown;
Already in the colleges the Word that was no word
Is processed from the podium by professors in prose,
And dedicated scholars in the graduate schools
Busy to squeeze the Absurd and divide the Void
Into courses given for credit, that the generations
May batten on the bitter diet of the desert
Until the secret desire of their blood shall be
To property protected by the blue police
Whose order guards the graves beneath the vaults
Beneath the banks, whose houses now are glass
Contempting stones; in whose aquarian light, subdued,
Glow golden secretaries inaccessible on stilted heels,
And savage action paintings hanging patient on the walls.

The Phi Beta Kappa poem at Harvard
15th June, 1965

A MODERN POET

Crossing at rush hour the Walt Whitman Bridge,
He stopped at the Walt Whitman Shopping Center
And bought a paperback copy of *Leaves of Grass.*
Fame *is* the spur, he figured; given a Ford
Foundation Fellowship, he'd buy a Ford.

THE DREAM OF FLYING COMES OF AGE

Remember those wingovers and loops and spins?
Forbidden. Heavy, powerful, and solemn,
Our scheduled transports keep the straight and level.
It's not the joystick now, but the control column.

THE ROPE'S END

Unraveling a rope
You begin at an end.
Taking the finished work
You pick it to its bits,

Straightening out the crossed,
Deriving many from one,
Moving forward in time
And backward in idea,

Reaching to finer elements
And always thinner filaments,
From rope to cord to thread
And so on down to splinters

No longer serpentine
That break instead of coil
And that will blow away
Before a little breath,

Having attained the first
Condition, being dust,
No longer resembling rope
Or cord or thread or hair,

And following no line:
Incapable of knot or wave
Or tying things together
Or making anything secure,

Unable to bind, or whip,
Or hang till dead. All this
In the last analysis
Is crazy man's work,

Admitted, who can leave
Nothing continuous
Since Adam's fall
Unraveled all.

PROJECTION

They were so amply beautiful, the maps,
With their blue rivers winding to the sea,
So calmly beautiful, who could have blamed
Us for believing, bowed to our drawing boards,
In one large and ultimate equivalence,
One map that challenged and replaced the world?

Our punishment? To stand here, on these ladders,
Dizzy with fear, not daring to look down,
Glue on our fingers, in our hair and eyes,
Piecing together the crackling, sticky sheets
We hope may paper yet the walls of space
With pictures any child can understand.

IN THE BLACK MUSEUM

When all analogies are broken
The scene grows strange again. At last
There is only one of everything.

This I had seen a long time coming
In my landscape of blunt instruments,
My garden of bearded herms.

For years I had carried a traveler's word
That he had seen in Fiji "sacred stones
That had children, but the children were stones,"

And did not know till now what silent thing
That hard, two-headed saying said: one mask
To every skull, that is the end of art.

These uncertainty relations now refine
Themselves toward ever-greater accuracy,
Unreadable in any antinomian sense,

Conceding nothing to a metaphysics;
As in my dream one night a sliding door
Opened upon another sliding door;

Or as two mirrors vacuum-locked together
Exclude, along with all the world,
A light to see it by. Reflect on that.

THE BLUE SWALLOWS

Across the millstream below the bridge
Seven blue swallows divide the air
In shapes invisible and evanescent,
Kaleidoscopic beyond the mind's
Or memory's power to keep them there.

"History is where tensions were,"
"Form is the diagram of forces."
Thus, helplessly, there on the bridge,
While gazing down upon those birds—
How strange, to be above the birds!—
Thus helplessly the mind in its brain
Weaves up relation's spindrift web,
Seeing the swallow's tails as nibs
Dipped in invisible ink, writing . . .

Poor mind, what would you have them write?
Some cabalistic history
Whose authorship you might ascribe
To God? to Nature? Ah, poor ghost,
You've capitalized your Self enough.
That villainous William of Occam
Cut out the feet from under that dream
Some seven centuries ago.
It's taken that long for the mind
To waken, yawn and stretch, to see
With opened eyes emptied of speech
The real world where the spelling mind
Imposes with its grammar book
Unreal relations on the blue
Swallows. Perhaps when you will have

Fully awakened, I shall show you
A new thing: even the water
Flowing away beneath those birds
Will fail to reflect their flying forms,
And the eyes that see become as stones
Whence never tears shall fall again.

O swallows, swallows, poems are not
The point. Finding again the world,
That is the point, where loveliness
Adorns intelligible things
Because the mind's eye lit the sun.

SUMMER'S ELEGY

Day after day, day after still day,
The summer has begun to pass away.
Starlings at twilight fly clustered and call,
And branches bend, and leaves begin to fall.
The meadow and the orchard grass are mown,
And the meadowlark's house is cut down.

The little lantern bugs have doused their fires,
The swallows sit in rows along the wires.
Berry and grape appear among the flowers
Tangled against the wall in secret bowers,
And cricket now begins to hum the hours
Remaining to the passion's slow procession
Down from the high place and the golden session
Wherein the sun was sacrificed for us.
A failing light, no longer numinous,
Now frames the long and solemn afternoons
Where butterflies regret their closed cocoons.
We reach the place unripe, and made to know
As with a sudden knowledge that we go
Away forever, all hope of return
Cut off, hearing the crackle of the burn-
ing blade behind us, and the terminal sound
Of apples dropping on the dry ground.

Two Girls

I saw again in a dream the other night
Something I saw in daylight years ago,
A path in the rainy woods, a shaft of light,
And two girls walking together through shadow,
Through dazzle, till I lost them on their way
In gloom embowering beyond the glade.
The bright oblivion that belongs to day
Covered their steps, nothing of them remained,

Until the darkness brought them forth again
To the rainy glitter and the silver light,
The ancient leaves that had not fallen then.
Two girls, going forever out of sight,
Talking of lovers, maybe, and of love:
Not that blind life they'd be the mothers of.

The Mud Turtle

Out of the earth beneath the water,
Dragging over the stubble field
Up to the hilltop in the sun
On his way from water to water,
He rests an hour in the garden,
His alien presence observed by all:
His lordly darkness decked in filth
Bearded with weed like a lady's favor,
He is a black planet, another world
Never till now appearing, even now
Not quite believably old and big,
Set in the summer morning's midst
A gloomy gemstone to the sun opposed.
Our measures of him do not matter,
He would be huge at any size;
And neither does the number of his years,
The time he comes from doesn't count.

When the boys tease him with sticks
He breaks the sticks, striking with
As great a suddenness as speed;
Fingers and toes would snap as soon,
Says one of us, and the others shudder.
Then when they turn him on his back
To see the belly heroically yellow,
He throws himself fiercely to his feet,
Brings down the whole weight of his shell,
Spreads out his claws and digs himself in
Immovably, invulnerably,
But for the front foot on the left,
Red-budded, with the toes torn off.
So over he goes again, and shows
Us where a swollen leech is fastened
Softly between plastron and shell.
Nobody wants to go close enough
To burn it loose; he can't be helped
Either, there is no help for him
As he makes it to his feet again
And drags away to the meadow's edge.
We see the tall grass open and wave
Around him, it closes, he is gone
Over the hill toward another water,
Bearing his hard and chambered hurt
Down, down, down, beneath the water,
Beneath the earth beneath. He takes
A secret wound out of the world.

FOR ROBERT FROST, IN THE AUTUMN IN VERMONT

All on the mountains, as on tapestries
Reversed, their threads unreadable though clear,
The leaves turn in the volume of the year.
Your land becomes more brilliant as it dies.

The puzzled pilgrims come, car after car,
With cameras loaded for epiphanies;
For views of failure to take home and prize,
The dying tourists ride through realms of fire.

"To die is gain," a virgin's tombstone said;
That was New England, too, another age
That put a higher price on maidenhead
if brought in dead; now on your turning page
The lines blaze with a constant light, displayed
As in the maple's cold and fiery shade.

from

GNOMES AND OCCASIONS

(1973)

Quaerendo Invenietis

I

I am the combination to a door
That fools and wise with equal ease undo.
Your unthought thoughts are changes still unread
In me, without whom nothing's to be said.

II

It is a spiral way that trues my arc
Toward central silence and my unreached mark.
Singing and saying till his time be done,
The traveler does nothing. But the road goes on.

III

Without my meaning nothing, nothing means.
I am the wave for which the worlds make way.
A term of time, and sometimes too of death,
I am the silence in the things you say.

Solipsism & Solecism

Strange about shadows, but the sun
Has never seen a single one.
Should night be mentioned by the moon
He'd be appalled at what he's done.

EXTRACT FROM MEMOIRS

Surely one of my finest days, I'd just
Invented the wheel, and in the afternoon
I stuck a bit of charcoal under the bark
And running it along a wall described
The cycloid curve. When darkness came, I sang
My hymn to the great original wheels of heaven,
And sank into a sleep peopled with gods.

When I communicated my results
To the celestial academies, sending them
Models along with my descriptions, and
Their emissaries came to ask of me
"What are the implications of the 'wheel'
For human values?" I was very lofty—
"I made the damn thing go around," I said,
"You fellows go and figure what it's for."

LINES & CIRCULARITIES

on hearing Casals' recording of the Sixth Suite

Deep in a time that cannot come again
Bach thought it through, this lonely and immense
Reflexion wherein our sorrows learn to dance.
And deep in the time that cannot come again
Casals recorded it. Playing it back,
And bending now over the instrument,
I watch the circling stillness of the disc,
The tracking inward of the tonearm, enact
A mystery wherein the music shares:
How time, that comes and goes and vanishes
Never to come again, can come again.

How many silly miracles there are
That will not save us, neither will they save
The world, and yet they are miraculous:
The tonearm following the spiral path
While moving inward on a shallow arc,
Making the music that companions it
Through winding ways to silence at the close;
The delicate needle that navigates these canyons
By contact with the edges, not the floor;
Black plastic that has memorized and kept
In its small striations whatever it was told
By the master's mind and hand and bow and box,
Making such definite shudderings in the air
That Bach's intent arises from the tomb . . .
The Earth, that spins around upon herself
In the simple composition of Light and Dark,
And varying her distance on the Sun
Makes up the Seasons and the Years, and Time
Itself, whereof the angels make record;
The Sun, swinging his several satellites
Around himself and slowly round the vast
Galactic rim and out to the unknown
Past Vega at the apex of his path;
And all this in the inward of the mind,
Where the great cantor sings his songs to God . . .

The music dances to its inner edge
And stops. The tonearm lifts and cocks its head
An instant, as if listening for something
That is no longer there but might be; then
Returns to rest, as with a definite click
The whole strange business turns itself off.

BRUEGHEL: THE TRIUMPH OF TIME

Passing a Flemish village and a burning city
possibly Babylon the Great, bringing the Spring
from Winter and any beginning to its end, there go
the actors in the ramshackle traveling show
that does whatever's done and then undoes it·
the horses of the sun and moon, stumbling on plate
and bullion, patiently pull the flatbed wagon
where Cronos munches a child and the zodiac-encircled world
bears up a tree that blossoms half and withers half;
Death on a donkey follows, sloping his scythe,
and last a trumpeter angel on an elephant
is puffing the resurrection and the end of days.

Under the wheels, and under the animals' feet,
palette and book are broken with the crowns of kings
and the instruments of music, intimating to our eyes
by means of many examples the Triumph of Time,
which everything that is, with everything that isn't,
as Brueghel patiently puts it down, exemplifies.

ZANDER ON GOD

It may not cover all theodicy
Or make him popular among the seraphim,
But "If God were true," my Zander said to me,
"He wouldn't make people not believe in Him."

ON GETTING OUT OF VIETNAM

Theseus, if he did destroy the Minotaur
(it's hard to say, that may have been a myth),
Was careful not to close the Labyrinth.
So After kept on looking like Before:
Back home in Athens still the elders sent
Their quota of kids to Knossos, confident
They would find something to die of, and for.

THIRTIETH ANNIVERSARY REPORT
OF THE CLASS OF '41

We who survived the war and took to wife
And sired the kids and made the decent living,
And piecemeal furnished forth the finished life
Not by grand theft so much as petty thieving—

Who had the routine middle-aged affair
And made our beds and had to lie in them
This way or that because the beds were there,
And turned our bile and choler in for phlegm—

Who saw grandparents, parents, to the vault
And wives and selves grow wrinkled, grey and fat
And children through their acne and revolt
And told the analyst about all that—

Are done with it. What is there to discuss?
There's nothing left for us to say of us.

OF EXPERIENCE

Nature from life by piece and piece
Gently disparts us; power fails
Before desire does. It needs not sex
To illustrate what Montaigne saith,
But only what's befallen X—
Now he no longer has his teeth
He can no longer bite his nails.

EPITAPH

Of the Great World he knew not much,
But his Muse let little in language escape her.
Friends sigh and say of him, poor wretch,
He was a good writer, on paper.

THE TAPESTRY

On this side of the tapestry
There sits the bearded king,
And round about him stand
His lords and ladies in a ring.
His hunting dogs are there,
And armed men at command.

On that side of the tapestry
The formal court is gone,
The kingdom is unknown;
Nothing but thread to see,
Knotted and rooted thread
Spelling a world unsaid.

Men do not find their ways
Through a seamless maze,
And all direction lose
In a labyrinth of clues,
A forest of loose ends
Where sewing never mends.

SEPTEMBER, THE FIRST DAY OF SCHOOL

I

My child and I hold hands on the way to school,
And when I leave him at the first-grade door
He cries a little but is brave; he does
Let go. My selfish tears remind me how
I cried before that door a life ago.
I may have had a hard time letting go.

Each fall the children must endure together
What every child also endures alone:
Learning the alphabet, the integers,
Three dozen bits and pieces of a stuff
So arbitrary, so peremptory,
That worlds invisible and visible

Bow down before it, as in Joseph's dream
The sheaves bowed down and then the stars bowed down
Before the dreaming of a little boy.
That dream got him such hatred of his brothers
As cost the greater part of life to mend,
And yet great kindness came of it in the end.

II

A school is where they grind the grain of thought,
And grind the children who must mind the thought.
It may be those two grindings are but one,
As from the alphabet come Shakespeare's plays,
As from the integers comes Euler's Law,
As from the whole, inseparably, the lives,

The shrunken lives that have not been set free
By law or by poetic phantasy.
But may they be. My child has disappeared
Behind the schoolroom door. And should I live
To see his coming forth, a life away,
I know my hope, but do not know its form

Nor hope to know it. May the fathers he finds
Among his teachers have a care of him
More than his father could. How that will look
I do not know, I do not need to know.
Even our tears belong to ritual.
But may great kindness come of it in the end.

On Being Asked for a Peace Poem

Here is Joe Blow the poet
Sitting before the console of the giant instrument
That mediates his spirit to the world.
He flexes his fingers nervously,
He ripples off a few scale passages
(Shall I compare thee to a summer's day?)
And resolutely readies himself to begin
His poem about the War in Vietnam.

This poem, he figures, is
A sacred obligation: all by himself,
Applying the immense leverage of art,
His is about to stop this senseless war.
So Homer stopped that dreadful thing at Troy
By giving the troops the Iliad to read instead;
So Wordsworth stopped the Revolution when
He felt that Robespierre had gone too far;
So Yevtushenko was invited in the *Times*
To keep the Arabs out of Israel
By smiting once again his mighty lyre.[1]
Joe smiles. He sees the Nobel Prize
Already, and the reading of his poem
Before the General Assembly, followed by
His lecture to the Security Council
About the Creative Process; probably
Some bright producer would put it on TV.
Poetry might suddenly be the in thing.

Only trouble was, he didn't have
A good first line, though he thought that for so great
A theme it would be right to start with O,
Something he would not normally have done,

O

And follow on by making some demands
Of a strenuous sort upon the Muse
Polyhymnia of Sacred Song, that Lady
With the fierce gaze and implacable small smile.

1. "An Open Letter to Yevgeny Yevtushenko, Poet Extraordinary of Humanity," advt.,
Charles Rubinstein, *New York Times*, 3 November 1966.

THE WORLD AS BRUEGHEL IMAGINED IT

The world as Brueghel imagined it is riddled with the word:
Whatever's proverbial becomes pictorial; if people habitually
Go crawling up a rich man's ass, they must be seen to do so
(through an orifice widened for the passage of three abreast;
The rich man, scattering coins from a sack, pays them no heed).
If people are in the habit of turning into toads without notice,
They must be seen to do so; if the owl is said to carry
Nestlings and nest upon her back, she must be seen to do so.

The world as Brueghel imagined it is hardly easier to read
Than is the one we glibly refer to as The Real World:
The proverbs get forgotten, or their meaning leaches out,
And in the unmoving frame all motions are arrested
In an artful eternity—the hay runs after the horse
Forever—so that we can't always tell coming from going,
Or literal good from allegorical bad, or arsey-versey:
The Cross may be headed for Hell, the pruning hook for Heaven.

But it remains, the world as Brueghel imagined it,
A plenum of meaning though we know not what the meanings are
In every place; and after having once experienced
The innocent and deep delight of understanding one
Or another emblem, acknowledging his just equation
Wedding the picture to the word, we take his word
In many matters wherein we have no further warrant
Than that his drawings draw enciphered thoughts from things.
So if the Ship of Fools is propped up on a pair of barrels,
Of if a man is shitting on the Beauty Shoppe's roof,
Or if Saint Anthony is somehow tempted (but to what?)
By a helmeted human jug with dagger and diarrhoea,
So that he has to turn away his halo and his head,
We get the picture, as we say, although we miss
The shrewd allusion to some ancient smart remark
That would have told us what we know and never say.

The world as Brueghel imagined it is full of decaying fish
With people in their hulls, it is centered on allegorical dames
With funny hats, who queen it over the seven deadly sins
And as many deadly virtues—the millinery architecture of Pride,
And silly Hope standing on water—: it is the world we know
And fail to know that he has seen for us and minded too,
Where from Cockaigne it's but three steps to Heaven or Hell—
Hallucinating, yes, but only what is truly here.

To D——, Dead by Her own Hand

My dear, I wonder if before the end
You ever thought about a children's game—
I'm sure you must have played it too—in which
You ran along a narrow garden wall
Pretending it to be a mountain ledge
So steep a snowy darkness fell away
On either side to deeps invisible;
And when you felt your balance being lost
You jumped because you feared to fall, and thought
For only an instant: That was when I died.

That was a life ago. And now you've gone,
Who would no longer play the grown-ups' game
Where, balanced on the ledge above the dark,
You go on running and you don't look down,
Nor ever jump because you fear to fall.

The Painter Dreaming in the Scholar's House

in memory of the painters Paul Klee and Paul Terence Feeley

I

The painter's eye follows relation out.
His work is not to paint the visible,
He says, it is to render visible.

Being a man, and not a god, he stands
Already in a world of sense, from which
He borrows, to begin with, mental things
Chiefly, the abstract elements of language:
The point, the line, the plane, the colors and
The geometric shapes. Of these he spins
Relation out, he weaves its fabric up
So that it speaks darkly, as music does
Singing the secret history of the mind.
And when in this the visible world appears,
As it does do, mountain, flower, cloud, and tree,
All haunted here and there with the human face,
It happens as by accident, although
The accident is of design. It is because
Language first rises from the speechless world
That the painterly intelligence
Can say correctly that he makes his world,
Not imitates the one before his eyes.
Hence the delightsome gardens, the dark shores,
The terrifying forests where nightfall
Enfolds a lost and tired traveler.

And hence the careless crowd deludes itself
By likening his hieroglyphic signs
And secret alphabets to the drawing of a child.
That likeness is significant the other side
Of what they see, for his simplicities
Are not the first ones, but the furthest ones,
Final refinements of his thought made visible.
He is the painter of the human mind
Finding and faithfully reflecting the mindfulness
That is in things, and not the things themselves.

For such a man, art is an act of faith:
Prayer the study of it, as Blake says,
And praise the practice; nor does he divide
Making from teaching, or from theory.
The three are one, and in his hours of art
There shines a happiness through darkest themes,
As though spirit and sense were not at odds.

II

The painter as an allegory of the mind
At genesis. He takes a burlap bag,
Tears it open and tacks it on a stretcher.
He paints it black because, as he has said,
Everything looks different on black.

Suppose the burlap bag to be the universe,
And black because its volume is the void
Before the stars were. At the painter's hand
Volume becomes one-sidedly a surface,
And all his depths are on the face of it.

Against this flat abyss, this groundless ground
Of zero thickness stretched against the cold
Dark silence of the Absolutely Not,
Material worlds arise, the colored earths
And oil of plants that imitate the light.

They imitate the light that is in thought,
For the mind relates to thinking as the eye
Relates to light. Only because the world
Already is a language can the painter speak
According to his grammar of the ground.

It is archaic speech, that has not yet
Divided out its cadences in words;
It is a language for the oldest spells
About how some thoughts rose into the mind
While others, stranger still, sleep in the world.

So grows the garden green, the sun vermilion.
He sees the rose flame up and fade and fall
And be the same rose still, the radiant in red.
He paints his language, and his language is
The theory of what the painter thinks.

III

The painter's eye attends to death and birth
Together, seeing a single energy
Momently manifest in every form,
As in the tree the growing of the tree
Exploding from the seed not more nor less
Than from the void condensing down and in,
Summoning sun and rain. He views the tree,
The great tree standing in the garden, say,
As thrusting downward its vast spread and weight,
Growing its green height from dark watered earth,
And as suspended weightless in the sky,
Haled forth and held up by the hair of its head.
He follows through the flowing of the forms
From the divisions of the trunk out to
The veinings of the leaf, and the leaf's fall.
His pencil meditates the many in the one
After the method in the confluence of rivers,
The running of ravines on mountainsides,
And in the deltas of the nerves; he sees
How things must be continuous with themselves
As with whole worlds that they themselves are not,
In order that they may be so transformed.
He stands where the eternity of thought
Opens upon perspective time and space;
He watches mind become incarnate; then
        He paints the tree.

IV

These thoughts have chiefly been about the painter Klee,
About how he in our hard time might stand to us
Especially whose lives concern themselves with learning
As patron of the practical intelligence of art,
And thence as model, modest and humorous in sufferings,
For all research that follows spirit where it goes.

That there should be much goodness in the world,
Much kindness and intelligence, candor and charm,
And that it all goes down in the dust after a while,
This is a subject for the steadiest meditations
Of the heart and mind, as for the tears
That clarify the eye toward charity.

So may it be to all of us, that at some times
In this bad time when faith in study seems to fail,
And when impatience in the street and still despair at home
Divide the mind to rule it, there shall some comfort come
From the remembrance of so deep and clear a life as his
Whom I have thought of, for the wholeness of his mind,
As the painter dreaming in the scholar's house,
His dream an emblem to us of the life of thought,
The same dream that then flared before intelligence
When light first went forth looking for the eye.

MYTH & RITUAL

You come down to a time
In every poker game
Where the losers allow
They've lost, the winners begin
Sneaking into their shoes
Under the covered table;
You come down to that time,

They all go home. And hard
As it is to imagine
A fat and rowdy ghost
Piss in his empty glass
So as not to miss a hand,
That's how it happens; Paul
Is gone, and Stanley is gone,

The winners have risen with cash
And checks and promising papers
And drifted through the cold door
Forever, while the host,
Like some somnambulist
Or sleepy priest, empties
Their ashes into the dawn.

THE RENT IN THE SCREEN

to Loren Eiseley

Sweet mildness of the late December day
Deceives into the world a couple of hundred
Cinnamon moths, whose cryptic arrow shapes
Cling sleeping to a southward-facing wall
All through the golden afternoon, till dusk
And coming cold arouse them to their flight
Across the gulf of night and nothingness,
The falling snow, the fall, the fallen snow,
World whitened to dark ends. How brief a dream.

SNOWFLAKES

Not slowly wrought, nor treasured for their form
In heaven, but by the blind self of the storm
Spun off, each driven individual
Perfected in the moment of his fall.

ANALOGUE

You read the clicking keys as gibberish
Although they strike out sentences to sense.
So in the fluttering leaves, the shoaling fish,
The continuum nondenumerable and dense,
Dame Kind keeps rattling off her evidence.

KNOWLEDGE

Not living for each other's sake,
Mind and the world will rarely rime;
The raindrops aiming at the lake
Are right on target every time.

from

THE WESTERN APPROACHES

(1975)

FUGUE

You see them vanish in their speeding cars,
The many people hastening through the world,
And wonder what they would have done before
This time of time speed distance, random streams
Of molecules hastened by what rising heat?
Was there never a world where people just sat still?

Yet they might be all of them contemplatives
Of a timeless now, drivers and passengers
In the moving cars all facing to the front
Which is the future, which is destiny,
Which is desire and desire's end—
What are they doing but just sitting still?

And still at speed they fly away, as still
As the road paid out beneath them as it flows
Moment by moment into the mirrored past;
They spread in their wake the parading fields of food,
The windowless works where who is making what,
The grey towns where the wishes and the fears are done.

STRANGE METAMORPHOSIS OF POETS

From epigram to epic is the course
For riders of the American wingéd horse.
They change both size and sex over the years,
The voice grows deeper and the beard appears;
Running for greatness they sweat away their salt,
They start out Emily and wind up Walt.

63

OZYMANDIAS II

I met a guy I used to know, who said:
"You take your '57 Karnak, now,
The model that they called their Coop de Veal
That had the pointy rubber boobs for bumpers—
You take that car, owned by a nigger now
Likelier'n not, with half its chromium teeth
Knocked down its throat and aerial ripped off,
Side stitched with like bullets where the stripping's gone
And rust like a fungus spreading on the fenders,

Well, what I mean, that fucking car still runs,
Even the moths in the upholstery are old
But it gets around, you see one on the street
Beat-up and proud, well, Jeezus what a country,
Where even the monuments keep on the move."

EINSTEIN & FREUD & JACK

to Allen Tate on his 75th Birthday

Death is a dead, at least that's what Freud said.
Long considering, he finally thought
Life but a detour longer or less long;
Maybe that's why the going gets so rough.

When Einstein wrote to ask him what he thought
Science might do for world peace, Freud wrote back:
Not much. And took the occasion to point out
That science too begins and ends in myth.

His myth was of the sons conspired together
To kill the father and share out his flesh,
Blood, power, women, and the primal guilt
Thereon entailed, which they must strive

Vainly to expiate by sacrifice,
Fixed on all generations since, of sons.
Exiled in London, a surviving Jew,
Freud died of cancer before the war began

That Einstein wrote to Roosevelt about
Advising the research be started that,
Come seven years of dying fathers, dying sons,
In general massacre would end the same.

Einstein. He said that if it were to do
Again, he'd sooner be a plumber. He
Died too. We live on sayings said in myths,
And die of them as well, or ill. That's that,

Of making many books there is no end,
And like it saith in the book before that one,
What God wants, don't you forget it, Jack,
Is your contrite spirit, Jack, your broken heart.

WAITING ROOMS

What great genius invented the waiting room?
Every sublime idea no doubt is simple, but
Simplicity alone is never enough.
A cube sequestered in space and filled with time,
Pure time, refined, distilled, denatured time
Without qualities, without even dust . . .
Dust in a sunbeam between Venetian blinds
Where a boy and his mother wait . . . Eternity!
But I am straying from the subject: waiting rooms.

All over the globe, in the great terminals
And the tiny rooms of disbarred abortionists,
For transport, diagnosis, or divorce . . .
Alas! Maybe this mighty and terrible theme
Is too much for me. But wait! I have an idea.

You've heard it said, of course, that anything
May instantly turn into everything
In this world secreting figures of itself
Forever and everywhere? How wonderful
That is, how horrible. Wherever you wait,
Between anticipation and regret,
Between the first desire and the second
Is but the razor of a moment, is
Not even time; and neither is motion more,
At sixty miles an hour or six hundred,
Than an illusion sent by devils to afford
Themselves illusory laughs at our expense
(we suffer, but they become no happier).

Think how even in heaven where they wait
The Resurrection, even in the graves
Of heaven with the harps, this law applies:
One waiting room will get you to the next.
Even your room, even your very own,
With the old magazines on the end tables,
The goldfish in the bowl below the window
Where the sunbeam falls between Venetian blinds . . .
And in the downstairs hall there is your mailbox,
One among many gathering paper and dust,
A waiting room in figure, summing up
Much in a little, the legendary box
Where hope only remains. You wait and see.

CRITIC

"I am self-evident," the mirror said,
"Plain as the nose on your face; plain as your face."

I unbelieving looked behind the glass
On razor, styptic, mouthwash and Band-aid;

And it has been my life's ambition since
To elucidate the mirror by its medicines.

NOVELISTS

Theirs is a trade for egomaniacs,
People whose parents did not love them well.
It's done by Wasps and women, Jews and blacks,
In every isolation ward in hell.

They spend their workadays imagining
What never happened and what never will
To people who are not and whose nonbeing
Always depends on the next syllable.

It's strange, and little wonder it makes them so
Whose lives are spun out talking to themselves
In allegories of themselves that go
Down on the paper like dividing cells

That form in communes and make colonies
And do each other in by love and hate
And generally enact the ceremonies
Intended to harmonize freedom and fate

Among the creatures and in the writer's soul.
The writer's *soul?* It's as if one abyss
Primps at the other's mirror and the whole
Shebang hangs fire while the lovers kiss.

THE COMMON WISDOM

Their marriage is a good one. In our eyes
What makes a marriage *good?* Well, that the tether
Fray but not break, and that they stay together.
One should be watching while the other dies.

THE WESTERN APPROACHES

As long as we look forward, all seems free,
Uncertain, subject to the Laws of Chance,
Though strange that chance should lie subject to laws,
But looking back on life it is as if
Our Book of Changes never let us change.

Stories already told a time ago
Were waiting for us down the road, our lives
But filled them out; and dreams about the past
Show us the world is post meridian
With little future left to dream about.

Old stories none but scholars seem to tell
Among us any more, they hide the ways,
Old tales less comprehensible than life
Whence nonetheless we know the things we do
And do the things they say the fathers did.

When I was young I flew past Skerryvore
Where the Nine Maidens still grind Hamlet's meal,
The salt and granite grain of bitter earth,
But knew it not for twenty years and more.
My chances past their changes now, I know

How a long life grows ghostly towards the close
As any man dissolves in Everyman
Of whom the story, as it always did, begins
In a far country, once upon a time,
There lived a certain man and he had three sons . . .

BOY WITH BOOK OF KNOWLEDGE

He holds a volume open in his hands:
Sepia portraits of the hairy great,
The presidents and poets in their beards
Alike, simplified histories of the wars,
Conundrums, quizzes, riddles, games and poems,

"Immortal Poems"; at least he can't forget them,
Barbara Fritchie and the Battle Hymn,
And best of all America the Beautiful,
Whose platitudinous splendors ended with
"From sea to shining sea," and made him cry

And wish to be a poet, only to say such things,
From sea to shining sea. Could that have been
Where it began? the vast pudding of knowledge,
With poetry rare as raisins in the midst
Of those gold-lettered volumes black and green?

Mere piety to think so. But being now
As near his deathday as his birthday then,
He would acknowledge all he will not know,
The silent library brooding through the night
With all its lights continuing to burn

Insomniac, a luxury liner on what sea
Unfathomable of ignorance who could say?
And poetry, as steady, still, and rare
As the lighthouses now unmanned and obsolete
That used to mark America's dangerous shores.

POCKETS

Are generally over or around
Erogenous zones, they seem to dive
In the direction of those

Dark places, and indeed
It is their nature to be dark
Themselves, keeping a kind

Of thieves' kitchen for the things
Sequestered from the world
For long or little while,

The keys, the handkerchiefs,
The sad and vagrant little coins
That are really only passing through.

For all they locate close to lust,
No pocket ever sees another;
There is in fact a certain sadness

To pockets, going their lonesome ways
And snuffling up their sifting storms
Of dust, tobacco bits, and lint.

A pocket with a hole in it
Drops out; from shame, is that, or pride?
What is a pocket but a hole?

THE DEPENDENCIES

This morning, between two branches of a tree
Beside the door, epeira once again
Has spun and signed his tapestry and trap.
I test his early-warning system and
It works, he scrambles forth in sable with
The yellow hieroglyph that no one knows
The meaning of. And I remember now
How yesterday at dusk the nighthawks came
Back as they do about this time each year,
Grey squadrons with the slashes white on wings
Cruising for bugs beneath the bellied cloud.
Now soon the monarchs will be drifting south,
And then the geese will go, and then one day
The little garden birds will not be here.
See how many leaves already have
Withered and turned; a few have fallen, too.
Change is continuous on the seamless web,
Yet moments come like this one, when you feel
Upon your heart a signal to attend
The definite announcement of an end
Where one thing ceases and another starts;
When like the spider waiting on the web
You know the intricate dependencies
Spreading in secret through the fabric vast
Of heaven and earth, sending their messages
Ciphered in chemistry to all the kinds,
The whisper down the bloodstream: it is time.

FIGURES OF THOUGHT

To lay the logarithmic spiral on
Seashell and leaf alike, and see it fit,
To watch the same idea work itself out
In the fighter pilot's steepening, tightening turn
Onto his target, setting up the kill,
And in the flight of certain walleyed bugs
Who cannot see to fly straight into death
But have to cast their sidelong glance at it
And come but cranking to the candle's flame—

How secret that is, and how privileged
One feels to find the same necessity
Ciphered in forms diverse and otherwise
Without kinship—that is the beautiful
In nature as in art, not obvious,
Not inaccessible, but just between.

It may diminish some our dry delight
To wonder if everything we are and do
Lies subject to some little law like that;
Hidden in nature, but not deeply so.

WALKING DOWN WESTGATE IN THE FALL

The weather's changes are the private rites
And secret celebrations of the soul
So widely now believed not to exist.
The first clear autumn day, the summer rain,
The sudden fall of winter and the dark
When daylight saving goes, the sunny melt
Of several February days, to these
Changes the soul with changes of its own
And overtones responds in resonance.

Down Westgate, in the fall, the housewives set
Chrysanthemums in bronze or marble bowls
Forth on the stoops, defying ice and snow
With their lion's mane, sun's face ruddy glow of gold.

Things like that marry weather with the soul,
Which would have its seasons if it did exist,
And sing its songs among the falling leaves
Under the autumn rain, and celebrate
Its mass with hymns and litanies of change,
Walking down Westgate past chrysanthemums,
Consenting with the winter soon to come,
Hearing the acorns bang on the roofs of cars
And bounce and roll along the rainy street.

THE CONSENT

Late in November, on a single night
Not even near to freezing, the ginkgo trees
That stand along the walk drop all their leaves
In one consent, and neither to rain nor to wind
But as though to time alone: the golden and green
Leaves litter the lawn today, that yesterday
Had spread aloft their fluttering fans of light.

What signal from the stars? What senses took it in?
What in those wooden motives so decided
To strike their leaves, to down their leaves,
Rebellion or surrender? and if this
Can happen thus, what race shall be exempt?
What use to learn the lessons taught by time,
If a star at any time may tell us: *Now.*

A COMMON SAW

Good king, that must approve the common saw,
Thou out of heaven's benediction comest
To the warm sun!
King Lear, 2.2.156–8

Had God but made me a religious man
I'd have it made. The suburb where I live
Affords an ample choice of synagogues
And seven different Christianities—

I'd go to all of them, to every one
In turn, continuous performances:
Confession and yarmulka, incense, candlelight,
High, low, and broad, reform and orthodox,

Allowing God no possible way out
But my salvation—save that God did not
Make me a religious man, but left me here,
From heaven's blessing come to the warm sun,

Twined round the pinkie and pinned under the thumb
Of Dame Kind dear and beautiful and dumb.

FIRST SNOW

for Ian McHarg

Always the solemnest moment of the year
Is this one, when the few first flakes
Come falling, flying, riding down the wind
And minute upon minute multiply
To being blind and blinding myriads.

It used to be said that when the sun burns down,
Being after all a mediocre star
Of the main sequence, mortal as ourselves,
One snow will seal the sleepy cities up,
Filling their deep and canyoned avenues

Forever. That will be the day. And for all
I know it may be true; at least it was
One vulgarized version of The Second Law
A century ago, and almost all
The celebrated authors did it up,

A natural: "London, Peking, Moscow, Rome,
Under their cerements of eternal snow,"
And so on; writing was a powerful stuff
Back then, and tales of entropy and The End
Could always snow the middle class. Meanwhile,
It only hisses through the whitening grass,
And rattles among the few remaining leaves.

CONVERSING WITH PARADISE

for Robert Jordan

To see the world the way a painter must,
Responsive to distances, alive to light,
To changes in the colors of the day,
His mind vibrating at every frequency
He finds before him, from wind waves in wheat
Through trees that turn their leaves before the storm,
To the string-bag pattern of the pebbled waves
Over the shallows of the shelving cove
In high sunlight; and to the greater wave-
lengths of boulder and building, to the vast
Majestic measures of the mountain's poise;

And from these modulations of the light
To take the elected moment, silence it
In oils and earths beneath the moving brush,
And varnish it and put it in a frame
To seal it off as privileged from time,
And hang it for a window on the wall,
A window giving on the ever-present past;

How splendid it would be to be someone
Able to do these mortal miracles
In silence and solitude, without a word.

THE THOUGHT OF TREES

It is a common fancy that trees are somehow conscious and stand
as the silent or whispering witnesses of the ways in which we bustle
through the world. But it is a truth of poetical imagination that the
trees are guardians and sponsoring godfathers of a great part of
thought. Not merely that various traditions have looked on trees as
sacred figures of the cosmos, as the source of moral distinctions, as
bearing all golden things, the apples, the bough, the fleece; but
also that trees, more than we generally allow, have formed our view
of the creation and nature of things, and, ambiguously responsible
for these, the mind's image of its own process. This we are told by
metaphors: a family tree, the root of the matter, a trunkline, a
branch of the subject, and so on.

Trees appear as the formative image behind much thought
brought to the critical point of paradox—

Where order in variety we see,
And where, though all things differ, all agree,

as Pope politely says of Window Forest. That trees, the largest
of living things, are initially contained in tiny seeds, is already a
spectacularly visible legend of the mysteries of generation and
death. The tree, rooted in earth and flowering in heaven, intimates
obscure and powerful reflexive propositions about the two realms;
that root and top strangely mirror one another deepens and
complicates the human analogy. The relation of single trunk and
manifold branches forms the pattern for meditation on the one
and the many, cause and effect, generality and particulars; while
the movement in three stages, from many roots through one trunk
to many branches, is supremely the image of historical process.
The tree's relation with its leaves translates the paradigm into
temporal terms, speaking of individual, generation, race, of
identity continuous in change, of mortal endurance threaded
through mortal evanescence, of times and a time.

Trees imagine life, and our imaginations follow as they may. The growth of a tree, its synchronous living and dying, from soft shoot to implacably hard (still growing) wood; the vast liquid transactions of capillarity within the solid form; the hard bark which nevertheless, as in the elm, reminds of water in its twisting flow; the enduring image of fluid life recorded in the rivery grain of boards (a mystical saying:—"Split the stick and there is Jesus"); the generalized simplicity composed of multitudinous complexity, generalized symmetry from the chaotic scrawl of upper branches; the simultaneity of freedom and order, richness and elegance, chance and destiny—these are some of the imaginings of the trees, which out of the earth and the air have dreamed so much of the human mind.

As architectural forms reflect their material origins, the first columns having been trees, so also with the mind. And so perhaps with its conclusions? "I shall be like that tree," Swift said to Edward Young, "I shall die first at the top." Since the eighteenth century, anyhow, when cathedrals began to remind people of forests and forests of cathedrals, it has come to seem sometimes that the mind acts in a drama staged with so high a regard for *realism* that the trees on the scene are carpentered at considerable cost out of real wood. Still, dryads and dendrones, the trees are within us, having their quiet irrefutable say about what we are and may become; how they are one of the shapes of our Protean nature, Melville in a single line expresses best—

The hemlock shakes in the rafter, the oak in the
driving keel

—and it is the founding tenet of poetical imagination that such images are inexhaustibly speaking, they call to compelling, strange analogies all thought that flowers in its fact.

DRAWING LESSONS

I

Your pencil will do particles and waves—
We call them points and lines—and nothing else.
Today we shall explore the mystery
Of points and lines moving over the void—
We call it paper—to imitate the world.
First think a moment of the ocean wave
When it stubs its toe against the scend of the shore
And stumbles forward, somersaults and breaks.
A moment ago nothing was there but wave,
And now nothing is here but particles;
So point and line not only turn into
Each other, but each hides from the other, too.
The seed of a point grows into a tree of line,
The line unfolding generates the plane
Of the world, perspective space in light and shade.

II

The points and lines, the seashore and the sea,
The particles and waves, translate as well
Into the consonants and vowels that make
The speech that makes the world; a simple thing.
Or else a complex thing proceeding still
From simple opposites that make it seem
As if it might be understood, though this
Is probably illusion in the sense,
Delusion in the mind, making the world
Our true hallucination. Much as matter
And anti-matter are said to explode at touch,
So at the meeting-place of sea, air, shore,
Both sides explode, the ocean into spray,
The shore more slowly into boulders, rocks,
And final sand. All this repeats itself.

III

Always repeat yourself. To draw a line
's not much, but twenty-seven wavy lines
In parallel will visibly become
The sea; by tempering their distances
Apart, now near, now far away, we make
Ranges of mountains standing in their valleys;
By arbitrary obstacles of shape
That will prohibit passage to our lines,
We make a fleet of sailboats or a forest,
Depending on what shapes we have left void.
We see that repetition makes the world
The way it is, Nature repeats herself
Indefinitely in every kind, and plays
Far-ranging variations on the kinds,
Doodling inventions endlessly, as the pencil does.

IV

We said the water and the shore explode
And then repeat; that's not quite the whole truth.
For water has the wondrous property
And power of assembling itself again
When shattered, but the shore cannot do that.
The Second Law seems to reverse itself
For water, but not for land, whose massive cliffs
Break into boulders that break into rocks
That then descend to sand and don't return.
While I've been talking, you've been drawing lines
With your pencil, illustrating what I say
Along with whatever else you illustrate:
The pencil lead's become a stub, its black
Graphite remains became the world you made,
And it will shorten when you sharpen it.

V

The Second Law's an instrument, we're told,
Of immense power, but there's sorrow in it,
The invention of a parsimonious people
Accustomed to view creation on a budget
Cut to economy more than to delight
At splendor overflowing every vessel.
Land is the locus of form and dignity
Disguising the way down to age and death,
Shameful decay, and dust that blows away—
See, rub your drawing and it smudges into dust,
Because your pencil is a citizen
Of the middle-class material world, designed
To be a minor illustrator of
What we become and what becomes of us.
The sea's little more mysterious than that.

AN ENDING

After the weeks of unrelenting heat
A rainy day brings August to an end
As if in ceremony. The spirit, dry
From too much light too steadily endured,
Delights in the heavy silver water globes
That make change from the sun's imperial gold;
The mind, relieved from being always brilliant,
Goes forth a penitent in a shroud of grey
To walk the sidewalks that reflect the sky,
The line of lights diminishing down the street,
The splashed lights of the traffic going home.

from

SENTENCES

(1980)

LITERATURE

Is in good hands, it is being written
By liberated sex-maniacs, psychologists
With an eye to higher things, and novelists
Convinced they are psychiatric social workers
With a mission to the slums of the human heart;
It is being written by disgraced politicians
From the safety of minimum-security prisons
With pastel walls affording them protection from
The lower class of criminal while they write
Of finding Jesus, Who has given them
The hundred-thousand-dollar advance against
The major motion picture soon to be made;
And now new generations of trained chimpanzees
Are manning their machines, moving their lips,
Coming along slowly, all thumbs and unopposable.

ADORATION

When I report at the funerals of friends,
Which happens nowadays oftener than it did,
I am astonished each time over again
At the fucking obsequiousness addressed to God:
O Thou, &c. He's killed this one already,
And is going to do the rest of us
In His own good time, then what in the world
Or out of it's abjection going to get
For either the dead or their smalltime survivors?
Who go to church at ordinary times
To pray to God, who does not go to church.

As for those masses and motets, no matter:
He happens to be tone deaf (or is it stone deaf?
My hearing's not so good either). But once in a way
The music takes me, if it doesn't Him,
The way Bach does the Et In Terra Pax,
Or Mozart does the Tuba Mirum, where
We doomed and damned go on beseeching anyhow.
Does He, when He hears that heavenly stuff, believe?
And at the Lacrimosa does He weep for us?
No end, my friends, to our inventiveness:
God doesn't matter. Adoration does.

ON THE SOUL

The prick was the priest that in the first place joined
In wedlock the heavy body with the light mind;
The prick stands at the head of every sect;
It is the prick that keeps saying "only connect."
The Dean of St. Patrick's had the word, if you'd hear it:
'The thorn in the flesh is become a spur to the spirit.'
The prick is the soul philosophers should have sought:
A kid can get a hard-on from pure thought.

MANNERS

Prig offered Pig the first chance at dessert,
So Pig reached out and speared the bigger part.

"Now that," cried Prig, "is extremely rude of you!"
Pig, with his mouth full, said, "Wha, wha' wou' 'ou do?"

"I would have taken the littler bit," said Prig.
"Stop kvetching, then, it's what you've got," said Pig.

     So virtue is its own reward, you see.
     And that is all it's ever going to be.

WRITING THE REALISTIC SHORT STORY

A smile exchanged between a man and a woman
Across the busy terminal needn't mean
That they will necessarily fetch up
Together in a double bed; it merely
Acknowledges the odds; but all the same,
Back at the motel in the middle of the night,
After the Steak Oscar with the King Crab legs
And the order of french-fried mushrooms on the side
With the obligatory Sangre di Cristo, pinpoint
Carbonation blinking at the brink, when he said
"May we?" and she replied "Mais oui," the two
Bilingual lovers learning to talk in forked tongues,
And when she stood there in the middle of the room
On her round-heeled stilted hi-come-fuck-me shoes,
"Yes," she breathed, "yes," her eyes jam-packed
     With stars and flowers and titmice.

Coming Home to New York When
It Was Said to Be Going Down the Drain

Descending over The Narrows and across
The great lady carrying her torch for whom,
We flew up river past the bankrupt town
Down to its last Almighty Dollar, turned
On a Hundred and Twenty-Fifth Street, letting down
The wheels and flaps, a pretty tense moment—
Maybe the runways had been repossessed
And towed up Pelham Bay? No, we got down,
And an hour later there we were again
Right in the midst of the biggest damn dream
Everybody ever dreamed at once, Manhattan,
Beautiful recipe for disaster, gone for broke
With half the money of the world in its pocket
And a hole in the pocket, the Port of Entry
And Zone of Interior for the lot of us,
The rejects the retreads the Four-Fs of every last
Country in Europe, our lot that grew up here
And sailed from here to knock the noggins off
Hitler and Mussolini and that mortal god
The Japs adored; and here it is, dead broke,
With lawyers from Albany to Washington
Screaming their parsimonious pieties
Against the wasteful ways of this Great Fact
That in the immortal words of Lazarus
Standing out there in the harbor, said
"Give me your garbage, send me whatever can walk,"
And made good every word, and, dying day by day,
Throwing the money away, made ruin renew.

THE THREE TOWNS

The Road from Adonoi to I Don't Know
Runs on, the elders say, to I Deny.
Whatever won't let us stop won't let us go.

The erected spirit, with its will to know,
Leaves the home town in its own good time to try
The slope from Adonoi to I Don't Know.

The slope so steep, it takes us who knows how
Further from God and closer to the sky;
Whatever won't let us stop won't let us go.

The elders warn, but it is always so:
The beautiful and brash are they that try
The road from Adonoi to I Don't Know

And sometimes in their brilliance mount up so
They finish further on in I Deny;
Whatever won't let us stop won't let us go.

The clear Satanic eminence of How
Runs further to the hermitage of Why.
Whatever won't let us stop won't let us go;
The road from Adonoi? I just don't know.

ACORN, YOM KIPPUR

Look at this little fallen thing, it's got
Its yarmulka still on, and a jaunty sprig
Of a twig, a feather in its cap, and in its head
There is a single-minded thought: *White Oak*.

Language and thought have changed since I was young
And we used to say it had an oak inside,
The way some tribes believe that every man
Has a homunculus inside his head.
Already, though, matter was going out
And energy coming in; though energy
Wasn't the last word either, the last word
Is information, or, more tersely, The Word.
Inside its dreaming head the acorn has
Complete instructions for making an oak
Out of the sun and the local water and soil,
Not to forget the great stretches of time
Required for cracking the code, solving the script,
Translating the sacred book of the white oak
With its thousands of annual leaves and their footnotes
—Amounting to millions in a century—
Instructing the oak in the making of acorns
And so forth and so on, world without end.

What the moral of this may be I do not know.
But once a mystical lady in a dream
Beheld her Savior, an acorn in his hand,
And asking what might this be was answered thus:
"It is in a manner everything that is made."

FIRST THINGS, AND LAST

So brief, so brave, so april pale
The little flowering before the leaves
Unfold themselves, the crocus opening amidst
The melting snow, the blue grape hyacinth,
Chalice of tulip swayed on slender stem—
Forsythia's yellow, watercolor-wet;
And sudden the sun's first warmth upon your face—

It makes us weep a bit for gratitude,
Poor foolish creatures we were doomed to be,
Born, as Augustine saith, twixt stale and stool.

There will be flowers at our funerals,
Pale flowers of spring, and, for an epitaph,
"They had a touch of class. But just a touch."

Morning Glory

Convolvulus it's called as well, or ill,
And bindweed, though sweating gardeners
Believe it rightly christened The Devil's Guts.

After it's tied whole hedges up in knots
And strangled all the flowers in a bed
And started to ambition after trees,

It opens out its own pale trumpet-belled
Five-bladed blooms—from white of innocence
Shading to heavenly blue—so frail they fall
At almost a touch, and even left alone
       Endure but a day.

During a Solar Eclipse

The darkening disk of the moon before the sun
All morning moves, turning our common day
A deep and iris blue, daylight of dream
In which we stand bemused and looking on
Backward at shadow and reflected light,

While the two great wanderers among the worlds
Enter their transit with our third, a thing
So rare that in his time upon the earth
A man may see, as I have done, but four,
In childhood two, a third in youth, and this

In likelihood my last. We stand bemused
While grass and rock darken, and stillness grows,
Until the sun and moon slide out of phase
And light returns us to the common life
That is so long to do and so soon done.

THE DYING GARDEN

The flowers get a darkening brilliance now,
And in the still sun-heated air stand out
As stars and soloists where they had been before
Choruses and choirs; at the equinox,
I mean, when the great gyroscope begins
To spin the sun under the line and do
Harvest together with fall: the time that trees
Crimp in their steepled shapes, the hand of leaf
Become a claw; when wealth and death are one,
When moth and wasp and mouse come in the house
For comfort if they can; the deepening time
When sketchy Orion begins his slow cartwheel
About the southern sky, the time of turn
When moth and wasp and mouse come in the house
To die there as they may; and there will be,
You know, All Saints, All Souls, and Halloween,
The killing frost, the end of Daylight Time,
Sudden the nightfall on the afternoon
And on children scuffling home through drifts of leaf;
Till you drop the pumpkins on the compost heap,
The blackened jack-o-lanterns with their candled eyes,
And in the darkening garden turn for home
Through summer's flowers now all gone, withdrawn,
The four o'clocks, the phlox, the hollyhocks,
Somber November in amber and umber embering out.

A CHRISTMAS STORM

All Sunday and Sunday night, cold water drops
At the will of heaven, freezing where it hits,
Glazing the windshields and the glistening ways,
Sheathing the branches and the power lines
In leaden insulations uniform
Across the counties and the towns, until
Connections loosen out and lines come down
And limbs that had sustained the horizontal
A hundred years unstrained crack under the weight
Of stiffened wet and short transformers out
So that ten thousand homes turned suddenly off
Go grey and silent, and the cold comes in
Slowly at first, then faster, drifting through
The window frames ghostly, under doors,
While night comes on and provident families
Remember where the candles and lanterns were
From last year, and other families don't;
While lucky families light fires, and others can't
But bundle up in blankets or skid downstreet
To the kindness of their neighbors or their kin,
And cars caught out are paralyzed at hills,
And it is clear that the relentless rain
Will go unrelentingly on till it relents:

Which it does do only next day at dawn,
When sunrise summons up the pride of the eye
To radiant brocades of fabergé'd
Drainpipes and eaves and scintillant fans
Of bush and tree turned emblems of themselves;
Where every twig is one and three, itself,
Its chrysalis in ice transparent, and last
Haloed in splintering light, as in the great
Museum of mind the million Christmas trees
Illuminate their diamonded display
To crystalline magnificent candelabra
Of silver winking ruby and emerald and gold
As angled to the sun by the glittering wind,
To show forth, to show up, to show off
The rarely tinseled treasures of the world
Before the powerful, before the poor.

CEREMONY

At five of this winter morn the hound and I
Go out the kitchen door to piss in the snow,
As we have done in all solemnity
Since he was a pup and would wake me up to go.

We mingle our yellow waters with the white
In a spatter of silence under the wheeling skies
Wherein the failing moon lets fall her light
Between Orion and the Pleiades.

WALKING THE DOG

Two universes mosey down the street
Connected by love and a leash and nothing else.
Mostly I look at lamplight through the leaves
While he mooches along with tail up and snout down,
Getting a secret knowledge through the nose
Almost entirely hidden from my sight.

We stand while he's enraptured by a bush
Till I can't stand our standing any more
And haul him off; for our relationship
Is patience balancing to this side tug
And that side drag; a pair of symbionts
Contented not to think each other's thoughts.

What else we have in common's what he taught,
Our interest in shit. We know its every state
From steaming fresh through stink to nature's way
Of sluicing it downstreet dissolved in rain
Or drying it to dust that blows away.
We move along the street inspecting shit.

His sense of it is keener far than mine,
And only when he finds the place precise
He signifies by sniffing urgently
And circles thrice about, and squats, and shits,
Whereon we both with dignity walk home
And just to show who's master I write the poem.

THE LITTLE AIRCRAFT

The little aircraft trudging through night, cloud, rain,
Is neither alone nor lost amid the great
Inverted ocean of the air, for a lane
Invisible gives it intelligence,
The crossing needles keep its heading right,
The neutrally numbering voices of its friends
Make of its blindness blind obedience,
From one to another handing its destiny on
The stages of the way with course and height
Till finally it's funneled in and down
Over the beacons along the narrowing beam,
Perfectly trusting a wisdom not its own,
That breaking out of cloud it may be come
Back to this world and to be born again,
Into the valley of the flarepath, fallen home.

THE MAKERS

Who can remember back to the first poets,
The greatest ones, greater even than Orpheus?
No one has remembered that far back
Or now considers, among the artifacts
And bones and cantilevered inference
The past is made of, those first and greatest poets,
So lofty and disdainful of renown
They left us not a name to know them by.

They were the ones that in whatever tongue
Worded the world, that were the first to say
Star, water, stone, that said the visible
And made it bring invisibles to view
In wind and time and change, and in the mind
Itself that minded the hitherto idiot world
And spoke the speechless world and sang the towers
Of the city into the astonished sky.

They were the first great listeners, attuned
To interval, relationship, and scale,
The first to say above, beneath, beyond,
Conjurors with love, death, sleep, with bread and wine,
Who having uttered vanished from the world
Leaving no memory but the marvelous
Magical elements, the breathing shapes
And stops of breath we build our Babels of.

By Al Lebowitz's Pool

I

Imagine this: three beach balloons of three
Sizes, sometimes spinning and sometimes not,
Float in the transparent water table
Reflecting light blue light up from the floor.
They slightly sink into their own images
Mirrored below themselves as bubbles a bit
Elongate gaining and losing their various colors
According as they move between sun and shade,
Shade of the sailing cloud, shade of the oak
And sycamore and apple standing over
Or bending above, and through the dappled light
Respondingly they drift before light airs,
Sailing in independence that is yet
Relation, unpredictable if not
Quite free, mysteriously going about
Their balancing buoyancies sometimes puffed
On some bits of V-shaped wake; like a mobile
By Calder, only more so—linkages
Invisible, of wind and the watching mind,
Connect and vary their freehand forms. The world
Is a misery, as it always was; these globes
Of color bob about, a mystery
Of pure relation that looks always right
Whatever it does. A steel-blue-black wasp
Rides on one ball awhile, flies to the next,
Possibly playing, possibly not; by law
Any three things in the wide world
Triangulate: the wasp, and Betelgeuse,
And Our Lady of Liberty in the harbor; if
It's any comfort to us, and it is.

II

Sunshine and rain at once, and the clear pool
At once lights up its light and shadow show,
Doing its freehand random perfect circles
That on a nucleus of bubble and drop
Grow outward and silently intersect
Without collision or consequence, as if
They lived between the spirit and the world,
And evanescing are replaced by others
In patterns that repeat themselves beneath
In light and shade that seem to ripple away
Between the surface and the floor and dazzle
Again against the sunshine side. Dame Kind
Is doing one of her mighty and meaningless
Experimental demonstrations, but
Of What? Playing, perhaps, with the happiness of
A couple of aperiodic crystals
Like thee and me, who are old enough to know
That if these moments could not pass away
They could not be, all dapple and delight.

III

Two girls in the pool, two old men out of it
Observing with an implicit kind of love
Mildly distinguished from lechery, much from lust,
The slender strong young bodies sudden as fish
To dive and swerve in the dazzled element
And surface (no longer much like fish at all)
Smiling, their long hair asparkle as with stars.
The old men, relaxed into their middle ages
And comfortable in the flesh for yet awhile,
Whom generation has had its will and fill of
And nearly if not quite let go, smile back
Over their drinks and banter with the girls
In a style that allows courtship and courtesy
To show their likenesses and keep their distance,
Just glancingly at risk; and the young women
Kindly respond in kind. No one, praise God,
Is going to get in trouble this time around.
It is late Sunday morning by the pool,
A Sunday morning late in summer time,
A Sunday morning of the middle class,
And no one, praise God, is even like to drown
Before it's time to go indoors for lunch.

IV

Likely the last of the summer's storms goes by,
And even the water in the pool looks lank,
With leaves already dead upon its flat
Spinning a while and sinking waterlogged,
A couple of struggling bugs doing the same.
Even the heat begins to ember out,
The year has perceptibly started down again,
And summer's wondering stillness is on the move
Over ourselves as well; a leaf comes down
And alights without a splash; another year
Of the little lot has passed, and what have we
Squirreled away more than this summer's day
With the electric storm hammering down on it
Releasing life? The banked furnace of the sun
With reliquary heat returns in splendor
Diminished some with time, but splendid still.
Beside the pool we drink, talk, and are still,
These times of kindness mortality allows.

V

An afternoon alone beside the pool
Observing, or more like peaceably taking in,
Recording, stillness made of rippling wave
And waving leaf, of shadow and reflected light,
And silence able to draw into its dream
The siren singing on the avenue,
The crying of a child two houses down,
The aircraft laboring through four thousand feet
On the way elsewhere. Stillness and silence still,
Shimmering frequencies of waterlight
Reflected from the planes of leaf above
And from the screening panels of the pool,
So many white oscilloscopes whereon
The brimming water translates into light.

Reflection and reflexion, lovely words
I shall be sorry to let go when I let go:
Reflected light, reflexion of the wave;
For things reflected are more solemn and still
Than in themselves they are, it is the doubling
Perhaps that seems to bring them nearer thought;
Could we reflect, did water not reflect?

Enchanted afternoon, immune from time,
Illusion's privilege gives me the idea that I
Am not so much writing this verse as reading it
Up out of water and light and shadow and leaf
Doing the dance of their various dependencies—
As if I might daydream my way again
Into the world and be at one with it—
While the shadows of harder, more unyielding things
Edge steadily and stealthily around the pool
To translate the revolving of the world
About itself, the spinning ambit of the seasons
In the simple if adamant equation of time
Around the analemma of the sun.

The Author to His Body
on Their Fifteenth Birthday, 29 ii 80

"There's never a dull moment in the human body."

—The Insight Lady

Dear old equivocal and closest friend,
Grand Vizier to a weak bewildered king,
Now we approach The Ecclesiastean Age
Where the heart is like to go off inside your chest
Like a party favor, or the brain blow a fuse
And the comic-book light-bulb of Idea black out
Forever, the idiot balloon of speech
Go blank, and we shall know, if it be knowing,
The world as it was before language once again;

Mighty Fortress, maybe already mined
And readying to blow up grievances
About the lifetime of your servitude,
The body of this death one talkative saint
Wanted to be delivered of (not yet!),
Aggressively asserting your ancient right
To our humiliation by the bowel
Or the rough justice of the elderly lecher's
Retiring from this incontinence to that;

Dark horse, it's you we've put the money on
Regardless, the parody and satire and
The nevertheless forgiveness of the soul
Or mind, self, spirit, will or whatever else
The ever-unknowable unknown is calling itself
This time around—shall we renew our vows?
How should we know by now how we might do
Divorced? Homely animal, in sickness and health,
For the duration; buddy, you know the drill.

ELEGY

My Thompson, least attractive character
Among the four because so fierce of character,
Whiny and scrawny, rolling on the floor
To be caressed, and scratching when you were,

There'll be three dishes now instead of four
Morning and night, and three to be let out the door
And in the door, and only you no more
Scratching the glass to be let in before,

All that about nine lives a lie, or else
One of the cruel deceits of fairy tales,
All nine bestowed at birth, and all the false
Nine taken at a stroke. Now what avails
Your caterwauling in that sightless See?
If Death should stroke thee, Thompson, scratch Him for me.

BECAUSE YOU ASKED ABOUT
THE LINE BETWEEN PROSE AND POETRY

Sparrows were feeding in a freezing drizzle
That while you watched turned into pieces of snow
Riding a gradient invisible
From silver aslant to random, white, and slow.

There came a moment that you couldn't tell.
And then they clearly flew instead of fell.

from

INSIDE THE ONION

(1984)

On His Own Terms

As with a liner at the speed of sound
Flying the sea, earth's weather left beneath,
All hurry is excluded from the hull
In streaming wind and night-shattering noise
And in the turbine blades that churn the cold
To fire and force trailing a ruin of smoke,

While inside, in low light, the master's moves
Are small and deliberate, their intervals
Quietly spaced as in recited rites
Traditionally prescribed by gravity
And far foresight; for certain that's the way
It is meant to be, one term of likening,
One term left out. So let it be that way.

Reading Pornography in Old Age

Unbridled licentiousness with no holds barred,
Immediate and mutual lust, satisfiable
In the heat, upon demand, aroused again
And satisfied again, lechery unlimited.

Till space runs out at the bottom of the page
And another pair of lovers, forever young,
Prepotent, endlessly receptive, renews
The daylong, nightlong, interminable grind.

How decent it is, and how unlike our lives
Where "fuck you" is a term of vengeful scorn
And the murmur of "sorry, partner" as often heard
As ever in mixed doubles or at bridge.

Though I suspect the stuff is written by
Elderly homosexuals manacled to their
Machines, it's mildly touching all the same,
A reminiscence of the life that was in Eden

Before the Fall, when we were beautiful
And shameless, and untouched by memory:
Before we were driven out to the laboring world
Of the money and the garbage and the kids

In which we read this nonsense and are moved
At all that was always lost for good, in which
We think about sex obsessively except
During the act, when our minds tend to wander.

IN MEMORY OF THE MASTER POET ROBERT BROWNING

Remembering that century and the one before
That seemed such inexhaustible springs of song,
Di quell'amor and *Dove sono* and the rest,
Orpheus wondering what he'd do without
Eurydice, the stuffed shirts in the stalls
Sobbing about Violetta, *croce e delizia*,
Coughing her love away, where did it go,
That wonderful stuff still with us now
But as a relic, the way they used to feel
Back then about Dreyfus, about Sedan,
La Gloire, Rhine Maidens with their swimming tits
Behind the scrim, now how could that have changed
And gone beyond our caring and our care?

When things are over that's what they are, over.
Master, I too feel chilly and grown old.
Like Ike said, he that conquered Europe, things
Are more like they are now than they ever were before.

IMPRECATED UPON A POSTAL CLERK

Nor rain nor snow nor heat nor gloom of night
Can stay this surly civil servant safe
Behind the counter from imposing his
Confusion, slothful rudeness and delay
Upon the simplest procedures of exchange.

May he bring his children up on Grade-B milk,
Continue less intelligent than lint,
Bid thirteen spades in No-Trump out of greed,
And have real trouble finding his own ass
With both hands and a mirror and a torch.

ARTHUR

First year of graduate school he's in my class,
Bitter and bright and breakable as glass,
Stage-nigger talk, like going on all fours,
Intention and effect quite clear: *up yours*,

Till I the man his teacher "Arthur" saith
"Let's keep our consonants while we have our teeth."
He did, although it took him several years
To talk like whitey even in his beers.

Two days ago he passed me in his truck
He used for plastering, painting, and "You fuck,"
He yelled, "How do you do these fucking days?"
And he had every consonant in place.

Just yesterday they tell me a heart attack
Took him, his fifth white girl is left behind
With infant *numéro* n; in the last sack,
Arthur, who learned to mind; but never mind.

At the Tomb of the Unknown Celebrity

You see how strange it is about the soul,
Hardly a one among the lot of us
Who witnessed his eccentric visit thought
Of him as anything other than he seemed,
Borne to us across an emptiness of space
And evanescing into it again
After the light went out, the lights went up,
Leaving us swept with empty empathy.

But now it turns out that he had a soul,
Or was one, dead in the middle of the way
Exactly, gone from the now here to the no where,
The undercover agent loved by us all
As by us all unknown, a stranger in
The unsuspected skin, his actor's art
Perfected to vanishing in the alien part.

Reverie of the Termite Queen

Sealed with my consort in the royal room
Under the hill that I have never seen
But made the makers of, I lie in state
While minions ply me with both food and drink

To cosset Majesty while I factor forth
The hundred million children whom I must
Outlive a hundred times before I may
Collapse the shrivelled whistle of my womb

At last effete and do what distinguished thing
One does to die. My proles, my infantry,
Parade on their endless errands hither and yon
Above my mystery, the soul of state,

Where I lie pulsing full with the ignorant host
That I dismiss into the world without,
Concerning which I am both dark and blind
As to what it may be, and why it is.

CALENDARS

At Christmas, for the New Year coming on,
The stores are colorful with calendars
To gift each other with, remembrances
Of time to come and to be followed through,

Appointments to be kept, accompanied
With moral maxims writ in ornate scripts,
With photographs of temples, flowers, tombs,
Endearing cats for those endearing cats endear;

Calendars thoughtful to companion us
With all conceits of Nature, Faith, and Art
Through all the seasons and the varied scenes
Where Time still begs his silent, sightless way.

POETICS

You know the old story Ann Landers tells
About the housewife in her basement doing the wash?
She's wearing her nightie, and she thinks, "Well hell,
I might's well put this in as well," and then
Being dripped on by a leaky pipe puts on
Her son's football helmet; whereupon
The meter reader happens to walk through
And "Lady," he gravely says, "I sure hope your team wins."

A story many times told in many ways,
The set of random accidents redeemed
By one more accident, as though chaos
Were the order that was before creation came.
That is the way things happen in the world,
A joke, a disappointment satisfied,
As we walk thrugh doing our daily round,
Reading the meter, making things add up.

GNOMIC VARIATIONS FOR KENNETH BURKE

*An answer can seem wholly radiant only with those for whom the
question itself has radiance.*

A Rhetoric of Motives

I

The only reason I'd care to be a king
Would be to hear the subjects speak their mind
And know that meant their minds belonged to me:
"The King's English"—imagine, owning a language!

II

The senses and the mind deceive each other,
So Pascal said, maybe remembering
The terse debate Democritus overheard
Between the two, mind claiming loftily
That sweet is by convention, cold likewise
Is by convention, while in reality
Nothing exists but atoms and the void;
To which the senses rise indignant crying
"Miserable mind! it is from us you take
The evidence with which you would destroy us;
Your victory will be your own downfall."

III

"Whatever the nonverbal, there are words for it."
        K.B., "Variations on the Word 'Providence'"

The Tao, the echoing spaces of a fugue,
The Cloud of Unknowing, The Clear Light of the Void,
Nothing to see but blind light to see it by;
Or else Nature going it on her own,
Blind mouths arranged in a fast food chain
With fucking to bridge the generation gap.

IV

When I first read Forster's famous battle cry
Only Connect, prefaced to *Howards End—*
Title designed as if to make me think
—I thought he'd meant to say "Only
Connecticut," but was interrupted by
A person on business from Cos Cob, because
The rebus represents Connect and Cut
Wedded and kept apart by Ego the I—
All dialectic in its nutmeg state.

V

My own small contribution to the great
Debate between the body and the soul
As to which should rule alone, is only this:
The lewdest image I was ever shown,
The filthiest suggestive pornographic piece,
Turned out to be an aerial photograph
Of sand dunes in sunshine and deep shadow.

VI

Between the senses five and Beldame Kind
Lies language, our fluid coupling with the world—
Incomprehensible, I hope you understand,
Because I said it plainly as I could.

We pause for these commercial messages:
"Man is the Cadillac of animals."
"The body is the Chris-Craft of the soul."
"The image on our new Phenomenal TV
Is so absolutely definite and clear
We can't even show it to you on your screen,
Which doesn't have the resolution, doesn't have
The definition, to do justice to
Its revelation of the empty eye."

VII

We have pursued the furious course of the world
As it ran from "If only . . ." to "If and only if . . . ,"
Kept faith with the author's egomaniac trade,
And followed the bedtime story of the world
Which may indeed have end, although so far
The children fall asleep before the end.

Kenneth, as you told me a time ago
How "We who used to elbow each other aside
Are closing ranks," now the fury of knowledge fades
And dialectic, if it do remain,
Remains the shell-game of its former self,
Unbeatable and obvious as language

Whose Gödelian and Delphic word has ever been
Don't look under the hood while driving the car—
May it be our hope appropriate to grow
Into the next phase as into the former ones,
And go upstairs about as often as down,
And to as many times a day as fro.

THIS PRESENT PAST

The tulip's cup falls open helplessly,
The redbud's petals are already dust,
The trees are dropping all their various dreck
Pertaining to generation; once again
The spring has gone, as we complain it does
Year after year, before we had the time
To take it in.
          But brief as flowering
Has always been, our power to attend
Is briefer by far, and intermittent, too.
We look at the iris, say how beautiful,
And look no more, nor watch the fail and fall
Of its bruised flags. So runs the world away,
As blown about upon the rainy wind
The keys of the maple's kingdom copter down.

A BLIND MAN AT THE MUSEUM

His wife is pushing a pram with twins before them,
He keeps in touch with a hand against her back,
And going sightless along the galleries
Listens to her mild voice describing things
While the speechless twins, like seeing eyes, look up.

They walk past windows giving on the past
Of grazing cows and crucifixions and
Self-portraits where the painter's mirrored eyes
Reflect themselves unseeing in the plane
Eternity of art, unable to look out.

A strangeness, just. But I imagined him
As having been, before he lost his sight,
Himself a painter, or if not that a great
Authority who has in his head by heart
Much that she reads the names, dates, titles of

To the twins who see but cannot know or say
The scumble of the black impasto'd skull
Behind all this, the agony of the eye
That sees the hand that acts but cannot see
Beneath the finish of the age, the art.

She sees. and says, they slowly push along
Between the walls, his hand against her back,
The seeing eyes, like pilot-fish, roll on,
A dumbshow of predicaments untold
Moving familiarly among the worlds.

GRAVEN IMAGES
for Jean Tucker

So many lightstruck likenesses there are,
Passport and portrait, postcard, even Art;
The news, the faces in the news, the ads
Inventing envy, there must be a great many
More than the number of persons now alive,
And maybe more than all that ever were—

Such stillness from such evanescence snapped
And shuddered by a falling guillotine
Across a glass—
                    The subjects taken thus,
To empty eternity exposed, have been
Developed by emulsions and by salts,
Printed in mummified facsimiles
And fixed by drying liquids in the dark-
rooms where their faithless ikons come to light:
The frozen sections through a living face,
The candid shots that paralyze the sea.

LUCRETIAN SHADOWS

Suave, mari magno turbantibus aequora ventis, etc.

De Rerum Natura

I

It's nice, when the wind blows the waves up high as hills,
To stand on shore and watch the ship go down
All hands aboard. Not that we wish bad luck
To any soul on earth; but it relieves
Our daily anxieties to see disaster hit
As long as it hits the neighbors and not us.

It's why we read the papers, watch the news.

II

Lying in bed, watching the morning news,
I saw how a cameraman by his good luck
Had got himself set up in the liner's bows
Just after she had hit a fishing boat
Which split and drew down under after it
A couple of fishermen in yellow slickers
Drowning as easy as falling off a log
And at light speed transmitted to the world.

The cold and tilting sea, blue black and green
With ornament of lacy silver spray,
The little yellow slickers sudden as dream
Appearing in the iris'd lens and then
Sudden as waking gone, the world and I
Snug as a bug in a rug and warm as a worm,
Warm as a worm in the compost heap in winter—

That's how things happen, they say. That's how it is.

FISH SWIMMING AMID FALLING FLOWERS

*comme le pan de mur jaune que peignit avec tant de science et
de raffinement un artiste à jamais inconnu, à peine identifié. . .*

On a ground of pale gold water of watered silk
The painter of a thousand years ago
Angled his wrist so rapidly and right
The hairs of the brush bent in obedience
To do the swerve and diagonal of these fish
Swimming in space, in water, on watered silk,
And stippled in the detail of their scales,
The pale translucency of tail and fin,
And dotted at the brush's very tip
The falling petals and the petals fallen,
And scattered a few lotus and lily pads
Across the surface of the watered silk
Whose weave obedient took all this in,
The surface petal-flat, the fish beneath
The golden water of the watered silk,

So that a thousand years of the world away
On this millennially distant shore of time
The visitor to the museum may stare
Bemused down through the glass hermetic seal
At the silken scroll still only half unrolled
Past centuries invisible as air
To where the timeless, ageless fish still swim,
And read the typescript on the card beside
That says "Fish Swimming amid Falling Flowers"
A thousand years ago, and seeing agree
That carp did always swim, and always will.
In just that way, with just that lightning sweep
Of eye, wrist, brush across the yielding silk
Stretched tight with surface tension as the pool
Of pale gold water, pale gold watered silk.

ADAM AND EVE IN LATER LIFE

On getting out of bed the one says, "Ouch!"
The other "What?" and when the one says "I said
'Ouch,'" the other says "All right, you needn't shout."

Deucalion and Pyrrha, Darby and Joan, Philemon and Baucis,
Tracy and Hepburn—if this can happen to Hepburn
No one is safe—all rolled up into two,
Contented with the cottage and the cottage cheese
And envied only by ambitious gods . . .

Later, over coffee, they compare the backs of their hands
And conclude they are slowly being turned into lizards.
But nothing much surprises them these days.

INSIDE THE ONION

Slicing the sphere in planes you map inside
The secret sections filled up with the forms
That gave us mind, freehand asymmetries
Perfecting for us the beautiful inexact

That mathematic may approximate
And clue us into but may never mate
Exactly: bulb, root, fruit of the fortunate fall
That feed us with the weeps and utter tang

Of the ovoid circles and the slipshod squares,
Triangles rounded at their corners, space
Geometrized resisting its geometry
Imperfectly, as it was meant to do—

Like stepping on a raft and rocking it
So that its ripples square the corners off
For just a second before the Mad Housewife
Soothes down the angles and bends them into curves

As worrying her secret might be known
And ours, empiric and its theory
Be one again, her crispen crystalline
Arithmetic raveled and riddled in Time,

Her rounding off and averaging out
That favors the evenses against the odds
And makes the onion, holding in our tears,
One and the same throughout the in and out.

SHE

So Dante exalted his Beatrice, a girl
"Of great beauty and utterly without charm"
Of whom his wife once wrote Ann Landers, Ann
My husband is a decent kindly man
Though on the road a lot, but has this thing
About a dame's been dead for half his life
He's writing this enormous poem about
And I want to know should I bring the matter up?
The wise woman answered Better leave it lay,
And added Gemma baby you need help.

So whether you call your girl O goddess or
You stupid cunt is some damn thing to do
With your psychology or how you feel
Or what she is or some other bloody thing
Nobody understands or ever will.
She is a point of faith, a mystery, and
Like God the Just she has a secret name
Distinguishable only to initiates
Muttering betsy clara jenny jane
In bed and childbed and the holy grave.

For ——, to Protect Her from Burns

You know, my dear, had we been born
   Three hundred years apart
The neither of us would have bothered the other,
   We wouldna' ha' gi'en a fart.

But thirty year's the difference, dear,
   And thirty year apart's
What we have got between us now
   Though not between our hearts.

It's stupid Mother Nature, dear,
   It's mocking old Dame Kind
That keeps the body growing old
   Without she keeps the mind.

Old age with youth will hardly sort,
   Though it's a dirty trick
Old age it is, where everything
   Gets harder but the prick.

First Light

Only for wanting to see the world made new
In every weather, growing its colors again
Out of the brown, grey, black, the muted flowers
In Lennahan's garden beginning to burn orange
And lavender and blue, the steady sequencing
Of green and yellow and red, green arrow,
Green yellow red again above the road,
With ritual precision and gravity
Asserting The City in its formal law
More powerful and pure for emptiness
Than in the later traffic of the day,
I walk out of darkness and into first light,
Patrol and precinct of the speechless ghosts:
An early worker, a late-returning drunk,
Four lonesome joggers slowly fleeing Death,
The Harvester delivering The Globe.

from

WAR STORIES

(1987)

To Joy Our Student, Bidding Adieu

Your friends, dear woman whom I never knew
But by the delighted kindness of your smile,
Impersonal but kindness and delight
Received and like a blessing on the day,
Had got accustomed to the thought of death
As age and preparation and farewell,
With things to settle, time to settle things
Before we left; now you've surprised us
As you had scarce the time to be surprised,
Leaving the company and the lighted room
With the wine and warmth and amiable talk
To go home in darkness, on the rainy roads,
To cross the avenue none gets across—

But suddenly, my dear, struck off the books,
Gone missing in the middle of the way
For time's remainder, such as it may be.
Remembering your smile, I wish that I
Had learned it better, and got it down by heart,
That no more lights the narrow hall of day
With all your troubled kindness, your delight.

Authorities

Commanders, and behind them heads of state,
Are said to care for and spend sleepless nights
About the children they commit to war;
You can't help wondering, though, whether they do

Or whether, were you safely in their place
Of power, as it's not likely you would be
Nor weren't, but it's allowed to wonder,
You might not say, "Poor bastards, little shits,

They never learned their history in schools
And now they never will, and cannot know
They are the hinges on which the oily valves
Of history will balance before they close

Upon our reputations now, our fame
In aftertimes, when children will be schooled
Again in truths belatedly belied,
To shoulder our burden and their hopeless charge."

ON AN OCCASION OF NATIONAL MOURNING

It is admittedly difficult for a whole
Nation to mourn and be seen to do so, but
It can be done, the silvery platitudes
Were waiting in their silos for just such
An emergent occasion, cards of sympathy
From heads of state were long ago prepared
For launching and are bounced around the world
From satellites at near the speed of light,
The divine services are telecast
From the home towns, children are interviewed
And say politely, gravely, how sorry they are.

And in a week or so the thing is done,
The sea gives up its bits and pieces and
The investigating board pinpoints the cause
By inspecting bits and pieces, nothing of the sort
Can ever happen again, the prescribed course
Of tragedy is run through omen to amen
As in a play, the nation rises again
Reborn of grief and ready to seek the stars;
Remembering the shuttle, forgetting the loom.

THE SHOPPING MALL, THE MORAL LAW

The mannequins, young visions of delight
Outfitted all for sporting and for sports,
Lean back a bit with breast and thigh outthrust
In lazily yielding postures that invite
Into their filmy designers' shirts and shorts.

To stabilize their stance and prop upright
These swooning figures of a plastic lust
And keep them coming to this pretty pass
Without arriving, a discipline of sorts
Makes sure each has a ramrod up her ass.

THE BLUEJAY AND THE MOCKINGBIRD

The mockingbird, knowing he owned the tree,
Flew close on the tail of an interloper jay.
Through and around they went one after one
With considerable skill not hitting a branch
Nor even it seemed disturbing a single leaf,
And neither left the precinct of the tree.

For all we're told of territoriality,
There was no pecking, they seemed to be having fun
Of a serious sort; at intervals agreed
Each one retired to a neutral branch,
Where the bluejay screamed and the mockingbird copied him.

DROWNING THE BOOK

"Life is hard. And then you die."

Now listen, Howie, if anyone ever read
Those little verses that you sometimes do,
It wouldn't have been because they wanted to hear
About age, old age, and illness, and the grave
Or all that there they know enough about
Without your help, without your dubious help.

There's but three steps from Milton back to malt,
And but three grains of salt with a peck of dirt
Between the elegant this and the silly that;
And the purpose of poesy, as all of us know
Without the sermon, is, by telling the truth,
To disintoxicate and disenchant
By lying like Homer taught us first to do.

You'll recollect what in this vale of tears
Is consequent, that there are girls in it
Lighting desires that a bachelor sage
Said God alone could satisfy (He sometimes does),
Moving the way they move in dithery
Delight, with the delicate bend and thrust
Of this and that about their splendid persons
Until they swell and cry aloud for corks
And fade into the light of common day
To start our burning busyness again—

And why would they give a fart in a high wind
When every wheel of this unwearied mill
That turned ten thousand verses . . . this living hand?
You made your bargain before you made your bed:
Lie in it still, as if you must you may.

The sentiment of the epigraph would have been unremarkable enough save that when first
seen it covered both points on a T-shirt. The known instructors, with a long life's gratitude,
are: William Shakespeare, T. H. White, John Milton, A. E. Housman, John Keats, W. H.
Auden, Aristotle for Homer, Henry Thoreau, Alexander Pope, William Wordsworth, William
Yeats, and, of course, John Keats again.

MODELS

I

The boy of twelve, shaping a fuselage
Of balsa wood so easy to be sliced
Along the grain but likely to get crushed
Under the razor when it was cut across;

Sanding the parts, glueing and lacquering
And pasting on the crosses and the rings
The brave identities of Fokker and Spad
That fought, only a little before his birth,

That primitive, original war in the air
He made in miniature and flew by hand
In clumsy combat, simulated buzz:
A decade away from being there himself.

II

The fuselage in the factory was aligned on North
So that the molecules lay along the axis,
Or so they said, to make the compass read
A right magnetic course; and after an attack

You headed the aircraft to what you hoped was North
And fired one more burst at the empty night
To set the shaken compass true again:
It straightened the molecules, or so they said.

The broken circle with the centered cross
Projecting the image at infinity
Quivered before him in the vacant air
Till it lay on the target like a haloing light.

III

And memory, that makes things miniature
And far away, and fit size for the mind,
Returned him in the form of images
The size of flies, his doings in those days

With theirs, the heroes that came out of the sun
To invent the avant-garde war of the air—
Richtofen, Rickenbacker, and the rest—
Where if you were shot it would be in the back.

Where the survivors, by their likenesses
Before and after, aged decades in a year,
Cruel-mouthed and harsh, and thought the young recruit
Not worth their welcome, as unlike to last.

Low-Level Cross-Country

for Brooks Baekeland

A railroad and a river and a road
Roughly in parallel though near and far
By turns and sometimes twisted in a thread

Three-ply with crossings-over, tunnelings-in,
And passing astern as soon as coming up,
With every slope and slippage of terrain—

And suddenly the town has been and gone,
The market square, the churches, and the schools,
The cemeteries and the swimming pools,

And out again, map folded on one knee
To read ahead, if there were time to read
With all the names aslant or upside down,

And over the rises and the deep ravines
Uncharted, lonely, still, and left behind
In the steady passage of the exercise

At the scope of speed and the escape of space
Down on the deck, perplexities resolved
Before they can be solved, and all the world

Flowing away the way it always does,
As if it were made of time, the thrice-wound theme
Of the railroad and the river and the road.

NIGHT OPERATIONS, COASTAL COMMAND RAF

Remembering that war, I'd near believe
We didn't need the enemy, with whom
Our dark encounters were confused and few
And quickly done, so many of our lot
Did for themselves in folly and misfortune.

Some hit our own barrage balloons, and some
Tripped over power lines, coming in low;
Some swung on takeoff, others overshot,
And two or three forgot to lower the wheels.

There were those that flew the bearing for the course
And flew away forever; and the happy few
That homed on Venus sinking beyond the sea
In fading certitude. For all the skill,
For all the time of training, you might take
The hundred steps in darkness, not the next.

THE WAR IN THE AIR

For a saving grace, we didn't see our dead,
Who rarely bothered coming home to die
But simply stayed away out there
In the clean war, the war in the air.

Seldom the ghosts came back bearing their tales
Of hitting the earth, the incompressible sea,
But stayed up there in the relative wind,
Shades fading in the mind,

Who had no graves but only epitaphs
Where never so many spoke for never so few:
Per ardua, said the partisans of Mars,
Per aspera, to the stars.

That was the good war, the war we won
As if there were no death, for goodness' sake,
With the help of the losers we left out there
In the air, in the empty air.

WORLD LINES

A War Story

And there I was, is how these things begin,
Doing my final exam, a solo test
Of navigation by dead reckoning;
If you got there and back, you had to pass.

I got there in good shape, a mining town
Far north of nowheresville, and had turned for home
When the cloud closed down and the snow swept in,
Nothing but speeding snow and darkness white,

But I found the spur of a railroad headed south,
The Iron Compass, the Lost Flyer's Friend,
And followed that at a couple of hundred feet
Until it tunneled into the side of a hill,

And there I was. What then? What happened then?
Now who was I to know what happened then,
A kid just out of school the year before?
His buttons and bones are somewhere out there still.

Memorial Day, '86

D-Day + All the Years

What Daddy did on Opening Day? Yes, well,
He led the squadron out before first light
Over the Channel as far as Cap Gris Nez
And turned to port along the Frisian shores
Up past Den Helder and Terschelling where
We had lost a few, and so on up as far
As the Bight of Heligoland and distant Denmark
Where Hamlet and the others used to live,
And so wheeled homeward on a parallel track
To land at Manston in Kent for an early lunch.

Pleasant and warm under the perspex canopy
Of the office fifty feet above a sea
Hammered and brazen as on the world's first day,
A peaceable morning. And the sky was blue.

And Daddy sitting there driving along
Under his silly hat with the stiffener out,
Wearing the leather gauntlets flared heroic
Over the white silk elbow-length debutante's gloves
They used to wear then whatever the weather was,
And more or less the way you see him now.

Remembering the Way

When you get to where you're going after dark,
To the strange house where a shadowy person behind
A lantern lights you to an upstairs room,
You drop your kit and undress in the dark
And haven't anything to do but sleep
Or fail to sleep until the dawn lights up
And you can see what you have come to, this
Bare room that will be your room from now on
With its one window opening out upon
The lawn and thence to the field falling away
To the river shining between the trees and last
To the hills that rise beyond.
                              It happened that way
During the war sometimes, when you were posted
To a new place and got there after dark.

The Shadow Side

The evening sunlight coming down the meadow
And slanting through the window strikes to light
A silver service that her father sent
Down from the Enlightenment and across the sea
To cast its complicities of light and shadow
On the white wall in halo and silhouette.

Some things remain the same, the silver bowls
And swan-necked coffee urn with the fluted sides,
But shift their shapes now as their shadows pass
Along the wall, while evening on the meadow
And evening in the room make indistinct
The silver highlights sinking into gloom

Until it is full night and the new-made widow
Remains unmoved and dark and derelict
In the museum of wreckage and regret
Left of a life subjected to earth's shadow.

THE AFTERLIFE

The many of us that came through the war
Unwounded and set free in Forty-Five
Already understood the afterlife
We'd learned enough to wait for, not expect,
During the years of boredom, fear, fatigue;
And now, an hour's worth of afterlife.

Fort Dix, there at the gate, boarding the bus
That let me off in Newark to catch a train
That took me to Penn Station and left me there
Once more the young man on his own and free
Without much money, and with not much to do:
The Gates of Paradise opened and let me out.

In the real one, as I understand it now,
They'll take you to a base camp far from home
And line you up for uniforms and shots
And scream incomprehensible commands
Until you learn obedience again.
It will feel strange at first. But so it goes.

IN THE BEGINNING

Thus Freud deposed about our infant state:
Omnipotent and impotent at once;
Wawl and it shall be given.

Though what is given is never what we want,
So we must wawl again. O chiefs of state,
Are you like this, like us in this?

And God, you holy terror
With the big bang for the buck,
Are you as ourselves in this also?

Like any terrorist making all things new
Including the freedom of the will and the huge
Unsuitable purple hat

Aunt Sadie wore to sister's wedding?
And this verse also, was it there
When the morning stars sang together

And the other celebrities shouted for joy?
And is that why the infant in the crib,
Bearing revenge's infancy, condemned
To suck his thumbs till able to bite his nails,
Hollered like Freud among the cattle and kings?

More Joy in Heaven

This bird that a cat sprang loose in the house,
Still flyably warm and wet from the cat's mouth,
Beat like a heart set fluttering with fear;
The bird's heart first, but ours beat after it.

Some comedy came of this, the saner sort
Opening doors, the others batting at cats
With brooms, or flying towels at the bird
To muffle it safe from enemy and self;

Who after getting confused among the drapes
And flopping back from a window, from a wall,
Found out the empty daylight of a door
Left open, and left, thinking the good thoughts

It would tell its children in our children's books
About an ultimate kindness to the world
Where once, in a legend of the Golden Age,
One ecosystem beat the other, once.

Two-Person/Zero-Sum

The serious boy playing himself at chess
Always contrives to win, but subtly enough
That his obliging loser across the board
Will never realize what made him make
The plausible insignificant mistake
That would lead to loss in a dozen moves or so.

Nor ever thinks to assign a face or name
To the invisible other who is always there
Accepting the consequences of his acts
In stoical silence, subtly playing to lose
To the self on the hither side playing himself.

Thus do they even to the end of life.

Theater of the Absurd

Strange is the show enacted in the cave
Alone, whereat the unassisted man,
Lying as dead, does nothing on his own
Yet is responsible for all that's done,

Inventing the music as he sings the song,
Author, director, playing all the parts;
Forbidden to applaud or fall asleep,
He is sole audience to the moving scene

He cannot interrupt, revise, control,
Only endure to the arbitrary end
And curtain-rise upon the other world,
Removing what he like as not forgets.

THE CELESTIAL EMPEROR

Against the invisible antagonist
Waiting across the squared-off court below,
The emperor plays chess with living men,
The pieces all convicted criminals
For economy's sake already sentenced to die,
Which happens to them as they're sacrificed,
Exchanged, or merely lost by accident,
The emperor's or his enemy's misplay.

The men go through the motions as they're moved,
Moaning or sighing as the gambit goes,
And some, that are left in play for long enough,
Become connoisseurs and critics of the game
With exclamation point or question mark
As they approve or disapprove the choice.
He hears them not nor heeds, but listens to
The music of his clockwork nightingale.

Immortally singing the fashionable songs
That imitate our planetary fates
Moving against a figured ground of stars
That are fixed and firm as he, and never moved.
So many destinies are in the world
That to each of them the appointed child is born;
Though God be dead, he lived so far away
His sourceless light continues to fall on us.

LANDSCAPE WITH SELF-PORTRAIT

A shading porch, that's open to the west
Whence the weather comes, and giving on a lawn
Won from the meadow where the hay's been baled
In cubes like building blocks of dusty gold,
And further down, through trees, the streaming creek
With three still pools by passagework
Of rapids and rills in fretted rhythms linked;

And on the porch the life-defeated self
And reciprocating engine of reverie
Translating to time the back and forth of space,
The foot's escapement measuring the mind
In memories while the whole antic machine
Precesses across the floor and towards the edge
And has to be hitched back from time to time;

And there to watch the tarnished silver cloud
Advancing up the valley on a wind
That shudders the leaves and turns them silverside
While shadows sweep over stubble and grass,
And sudden the heavy silver of the first
Raindrops blown slanting in and summer cold
And turning continuous in silver strings;

And after that, the clarified serene
Of the little of daylight that remains to make
Distinct the details of the fading sight:
The laddered blue on blue of the bluejay's tail,
The sweeping swallows low above the swale
Among the insect victims as they rise
To be picked off, and peace is satisfied.

TRYING CONCLUSIONS

(1987–91)

LONG DISTANCE

Here on the phone is Miss Patricia Mitchell
Of Nacogdoches, Texas, who is writing her term paper
About a poem of mine she wants to ask about.
"It's such a privilege, Mr. N," she says,
Just to pick up the phone and talk to you.

"The others in the class are writing theirs
On Wm B Yeats and Emily Dickinson,
And they can't just call up and talk to them,
Now can they?" "No, Patricia," I reply,
"Now that you mention it, I guess they can't."

I've rarely felt so grateful to be in the Book
As I am talking with Miss Patricia Mitchell
Far out in faraway Texas, and not to be
Cut off and isolate, like William Y
and Emily D with their unlisted numbers.

MAGNITUDES

Earth's Wrath at our assaults is slow to come
But relentless when it does. It has to do
With catastrophic change, and with the limit
At which one order more of Magnitude
Will bring us to a qualitative change
And disasters drastically different
From those we daily have to know about.

141

As with the speed of light, where speed itself
Becomes a limit and an absolute;
As with the splitting of the atom
And a little later of the nucleus;
As with the millions rising into billions—
The piker's kind in terms of money, yes,
But a million^2 in terms of time and space
As the universe grew vast while the earth
Our habitat diminished to the size
of a billiard ball, both relative
To the cosmos and to the numbers of ourselves,
The doubling numbers, the earth could accommodate.

We stand now in the place and limit of time
Where hardest knowledge is turning into dream,
And nightmares still contained in sleeping dark
Seem on the point of bringing into day
The sweating panic that starts the sleeper up.
One or another nightmare may come true,
And what to do then? What in the world to do?

To the Congress of the United States, Entering Its Third Century

because reverence has never been america's thing,
    this verse in your honor will not begin "o thou."
but the great respect our country has to give
may you all continue to deserve, and have.

*   *   *

here at the fulcrum of us all,
the feather of truth against the soul
is weighed, and had better be found to balance
lest our enterprise collapse in silence.

142

for here the million varying wills
get melted down, get hammered out
until the movie's reduced to stills
that tell us what the law's about.

conflict's endemic in the mind:
your job's to hear it in the wind
and compass it in opposites,
and bring the antagonists by your wits

to being one, and that the law
thenceforth, until you change your minds
against and with the shifting winds
that this and that way blow the straw.

so it's a republic, as Franklin said,
if you can keep it; and we did
thus far, and hope to keep our quarrel
funny and just, though with this moral:—

praise without end for the go-ahead zeal
of whoever it was invented the wheel;
but never a word for the poor soul's sake
that thought ahead, and invented the brake.

26 ii 89

WITNESSING THE LAUNCH OF THE SHUTTLE ATLANTIS

So much of life in the world is waiting, that
This day was no exception, so we waited
All morning long and into the afternoon.
I spent some of the time remembering
Dante, who did the voyage in the mind
Alone, with no more nor heavier machinery
Than the ghost of a girl giving him guidance;

And wondered if much was lost to gain all this
New world of engine and energy, where dream
Translates into deed. But when the thing went up
It was indeed impressive, as if hell
Itself opened to send its emissary
In search of heaven or "the unpeopled world"
(thus Dante of doomed Ulysses) "behind the sun."

So much of life in the world is memory
That the moment of the happening itself—
So rich with noise and smoke and rising clear
To vanish at the limit of our vision
Into the light blue light of afternoon—
Appeared no more, against the void in aim,
Than the flare of a match in sunlight, quickly snuffed.

What yet may come of this? We cannot know.
Great things are promised, as the promised land
Promised to Moses that he would not see
But a distant sight of, though the chidren would.
The world is made of pictures of the world,
And the pictures change the world into another world
We cannot know, as we knew not this one.

THE PROCESS

Every four years or every eight,
A dozen gents and maybe a couple of dames
Announce they have received the money and the Word
That fits them for the highest office in the land.
And so begins The Process,

With winnowing and sorting, winter to spring
With travel and talk and too much chicken à la king,
Till by the summer's end but two remain
To take the road again,

Traducing each other's patriotism, race,
And putative paternity, with one hand out
For the money the other throws away
On balloons and signs and party favors,

Till come November the survivor is allowed to say
That providence, and guidance divine,
Have brought him to the highest office in the land
And the greatest power ever known on earth,

Where he will be advised by expertise,
Instructed what to say and how to smile
While saying it; where he will be cartooned
And told to do this and that until
He either does it or he doesn't.

For this he gets to live in a grand house
Infiltrated by a thousand tourists in a day
And overseen by servants, while the same
Vain music is played wherever he walks—

Such is The Process, concerning which a couple of drunks
In a bar the next night after Election Day
Challenged each other to say the Pledge
Of Allegiance they had had to learn at school;

And one drunk said "Mine eyes have seen
The Glory of the coming of the Lord,"
And the other said "from sea to shining sea,"
And the first drunk said "you said it, Jack."

MEDIA

The TV has been showing movies of dead poets
lately, they come on once a week or so,
movies mostly of stills of the dead poets,
the passport photographs, the family groups
with the child poet circled in sepia ink.

145

The black and white poets are read and discussed
by poets in living color, though some have died since.
The camera doesn't always know what to do
while the poems are being read, but drifts
across a crowd of faces or a rural scene
or waves breaking in splash and spray
against black rocks and leaving a shampoo of foam;
sometimes referring to the words that are being said,
oftener not, but always in images poetical
suggestive of the well-loved themes of poetry,
nature and innocence and cruel indifference,
sorrow, and memories cemetery-still,

while the living poets read and interrupt
the reading with reminiscences of praise
and remarks interpretive about the dead poets
whose transitive poems are being printed out
across the screen, across the crowd of faces,
and all is again as though it had never been.

ANSWERING BACK

*"Does the imagination dwell the most
Upon a woman won or a woman lost?"*
                                    —W. B. Yeats

You silly Willie, on the woman lost.
The woman won sits in the inglenook
Across from you, knitting or reading a book
Or come your teatime doing the toast and bacon;
Whereas the woman lost is God knows where
In the world, and with whom, if not by now a ghost
Past yours or anyone's love, though still you care
Lest she be by another bespoken or taken—
For what's romantic love unless forsaken?

SOUNDINGS

I

Watching the TV with the sound turned off
May seem a foolish exercise enough
To them that haven't tried it, and to them that won't.
But as one or another philosopher may have said,
"There's nothing so stupid I can't learn from it,"
And once or twice I've found its speechlessness
Instructive, leading on to memories
And thoughts, and thence to dreams and dreamless sleep.

II

First off, the essential nonsense of a world
Deprived of its word is depicted as in high relief
By the gesturing figures with their writhing lips
Playing at kindness and wrath, as in the ads
That make a virtue of mendacity,
Where the fake food is forked into the mouths
That smile while chewing, quite a trick, and then expel
In strange contortions syllables unvoiced,
Unbreathed—
        till you remember your childhood, and are
Even reminded of unremembered infancy
With the grown-ups huge as pharaonic stones
Bending above you and grimacing their mouths
To make the sounds you wouldn't understand
Till your language grew—
        which led in turn to thoughts
Of the Cave that Socrates told us about
So long ago in our freshman year at school,
The stepwise allegory that described
To the children of this world what it might mean
To become children of light—
        which brings me back
To these children of light the screen displays,
Shadows cavorting in color and mouthing the words
That fail to incarnate or are stillborn.

III

I thought to say, "They're actors, it's all an act,"
But must have fallen asleep, for I heard in my dream
An astronomical sentence I had read:
"Every red giant has a white dwarf at its core,
And the white dwarf eats the red giant in the end,"
Which now the dream interpreted to mean
That every Goliath has a David in his heart,
But it still takes a rock and a sling to bring him down.

IV

When I awakened, it was very late,
Programs were over for the night, we were
No longer programmed, and the screen was filled
With flakes of snow that danced but never fell
And, dazzling the eyes, dizzied the mind.
I went over to the window to see if snow
Was falling (no), turned off the set and so
Upstairs to bed with, first, a memory
Of that miracle of the high school physics class,
The oscilloscope that translated sound to sight,
And of the musical score, that for the instructed
Did the same thing, but this time in reverse.

There came these thoughts, residues of the dream
Or canonical variations on its theme:

"The lightning writes the lines against the night
For thunder the loud buffoon to bellow aloud."

"It is the still and sky-reflecting pool
Whose gravity powers the chattering waterfall."

And last: "The essential human statement is
'I give you my word.' This is the bottom line."

ROMANTICS

Such as it seemed to them, well, so it seemed,
And as it seems now at a later time
Theirs wasn't quite the thing we would have aimed
To be remembered by, the mirroring chime

We made with Nature, and Nature made with us.
Nor poison ivy, acne, nor the gout
Their nature coped not with; ridiculous
And brave they were; we honor them with doubt.

REALISTS

A wolf stood over the corpse of a throat-torn sheep,
and all of us in the exhibition hall
pitied the sheep. We continued pitiful
After it came to us that wolf and sheep
Were part of the show, and stuffed with the same wool.

MINIMS (1–6)

EPITAPH ON A SCHOOL OF FICTION

They wrote about what they knew. It didn't take long.

SPRING

Bees to the Flowers, Flies to Shit.

A LONG FAREWELL

Goodbye, said the river, I'm going downstream.

A DOUBLE CROSS

Early in life and late, at both ends cozen'd:
The girls were chaste, when he was young and wasn't.

149

AESTHETICS

The spider does geometry all night
To take the fly, the dewdrop, and the sun's light.

FINANCING THE FAIRY TALE WITH A HAPPY ENDING

Miss Piggy and Kermit the Frog
Have merged with Mickey and Minnie.
They will live by the sea in the smog,
And always have plenty of money.

THE REVISED VERSION

The common curse forbidden to the young
When we were young—our grown-ups got it wrong,
Maybe from reading in a bad translation;

It wasn't so much a curse as an invitation
To the great world's permanent floating cocktail bash—
The scent, the smoke, the burning, and the ash.

A grown-up in my turn I say the spell:
It isn't Go to Hell, it's Come to Hell.

ANALOGIES

In Memory of William Empson

Where the abscissa and the ordinate meet,
Where every value sums to zero as
The sand wastes into the waist of the hourglass
Till all the signs no longer signify
And the cardinal points, under a spinning sun,
Become equivalent, at the Judgment Day
Which never will be though it always is—

To the point of that top the universe
Is spinning away, and yet, so vast it is,
It's able to pulley up almost its own weight
On the primrose path, and order on the way
Mosquito and music and many great things else
Beïore it falls into its vanishing point
Where the abscissa and the ordinate meet.

1776

The stars—what do they Burn—
Do they have "atmosphere"?
Or journey 'round the Horn
    Or past Cape Fear?

Let distances of Earth
Sublime themselves to Them—
As people do—in Church—
The dusty copper glint—of Mars.

LARKIN

Imagine Larkin going among the dead,
Not yet at home there, as he wasn't here,
And doing them the way he did *The Old Fools*,
With edged contempt becoming sympathy
Of a sort, and sympathy contempt for death.

It's a quirky spirit he carried through the arch
To aftertime, making a salted fun
Of all the show and grudging his respect
For all but truth, the master of a style
Able to see things as he saw through things.

He was our modern; in his attitude,
And not in all that crap about free verse.
He understood us, not as we would be
Understood in smartass critical remarks,
But as we are when we stand in our shoes and say.

Our Roman, too; he might not have cared to be,
But what I mean is this: you wander through
The galleries entranced with shepherdess and nymph,
The marble or alabaster faery and fay,
Then suddenly you come on him, the stone

Of his face scored up and scarred with the defeat
An honorable life has brought him to,
And know that backing up the tales we tell
Is mortal this, the what-it's-all-about,
So that you turn away, the lesson told,

That's it. Dear Warlock-Williams, might you weep?
The penetrative emptiness of that gaze
Kindly accusing none, forgiving none,
Is just the look upon the face of truth,
Mortality knowing itself as told to do,

And death the familiar comes as no surprise—
"Ah, Warlock-Williams, are you here as well?"
With Auden, with Hardy, with the other great and dead,
Dear Larkin of the anastrophic mind,
Forever now among the undeceived.

THE FORBIDDEN CITY

When the youths and maidens had been sacrificed
And their burned bodies bundled away by night,
The mediate mind erased their images,
Replacing what the witnesses said they saw
With memories preferred by the regime.

The world well knew it listened to a lie
Made up of lies, but nodded its great head
Globular and said it was the way of the world
To know the truth and prefer to be deceived,
Smoothed over and soothed in cynical innocence,

No matter what Cassandra cried, whose curse
Was to tell the truth and never be believed;
One hand will wash the other, never mind
If waterish indifference disregard
What resentment implacable bakes sour and hard.

THE EVERGREEN

We light the tree tonight,
Encouraging the sun
To bring the world back up
Out of December's dark.

We do this every year,
Our homely miracle
Wrought out of strong good will
So far has never failed;

Nor may it ever fail,
This light that is sent forth
Whenever a child is born,
To burn the night away

And start in joy again
The story of the world;
Though knowing, as we do,
Its ending in grief and spring.

WASTE

The glittering burial mound of flattened cars,
Some few of them spattered inside with blood,
And on the other side of the soaring bridge
On the way to the airport, the cracking plants,
Tall silver candles flaming at their tips
While they refine the fuel of fresh desires—

Riding between petroleum and rust
To rise above our little lives awhile
And see the cities and the parking lots
From high above as the gods used to do,
Or as cryptic patterns made of beaded lights,
An everlasting Christmas tree of life—

Till the aircraft meets its shadow once again
And we are as we were, in another town
Not much unlike the one we thought we had left,
Ourselves the same selves we had left behind
Reduced again into the plane of love
And fear and all-obligatory guilt—

There is no end to the loves we flew to meet,
The funerals duty bound us to attend
At energies that never were till now
And quivering anxieties also new
In their pitch of tension and discontent
And impatience to be getting there, but where?

Now in the taxi into town we pass
Again, as if it were another life
Reviewed, the heaped up mass of rusting cars
And on the other side of the soaring bridge
The cracking plants, the candles of desire
That lead us on to unconsidered ends—

Our destinations being destinies,
Because we lust and fear and worry about
Our lust and fear and what the future holds
For us who waste the world while doing time,
Making the babies, attending the funerals,
Cutting the deals, catching the next flight out.

A Keepsake for the Kids

Now if they'd told you in your twentieth year
The true prudential meaning of *wedlock:*
To keep the property with propriety
And see succession kept legitimate,
Not keep the bastards seeded in the field
Until they climbed to claim preeminence;

And if they'd told you that your faraway death
Foreseen was meant to stabilize order divine
Upon the earth, whereto both church and state
Contributed your widow's mite, and keep
The rich in their high penthouses pent,
The poor stuck by their soles to the dirt beneath,

What could you have said to that but No in spades?
For you were twenty, remember? and in love?

155

AUGUST

The bow of the sun by now less strongly bent,
Summer's retreat along the Zodiac Line
Has plainly begun, but still the drought and heat
Of its holding action keep up the hopeless fight
With unforgiving fire which we endure
Because we must and cannot but; like troops
Entrenched, who, told of an armistice to come,
Keep their heads down and shelter in the lines
And sullenly resent, sometimes refuse,
An order into action—so do we
Cower indoors and try to keep our cool
And undertake no novel enterprise
Till better times, as promised, be at hand;
Each one of us thinking what a fool he'd be
To be the last one killed before the peace
With Summer is signed, before the Fall.

KICKING OFF THE COMBINED FEDERAL CAMPAIGN, OCTOBER 11, 1988

We who survived the IRS once more
At planting time last April, we citizens
Who coughed until we brought the money up
To go to hidden coffers and designs,
Are being asked, now that the harvest's here,
To tithe once more, and of our own sweet will.

It's tough, and no doubt tougher than enough,
To be brought in to bring our wallets out
To give for once instead of being taken;
But there's a difference that signifies:
We're doing it ourselves, and where it counts,
To help the helpless, who cannot help themselves.

Out at Free Enterprise, where the Needies fight
The Greedies for the great Grail of the World
And always lose, we can help to balance up
The scales of earthly good; not much, but some;
And for a wonder, though it hurt at first,
It will feel good because our kindness did it.

Remember, if it hurts, our kindness does it,
And kindness a little bit restores the world
To what it might be, what it ought to be,
By a little and a little at a time—
Money like muck Sir Francis Bacon said,
        No good but it be spread.

THE AMATEURS OF HEAVEN

to Frances

Two lovers to a midnight meadow came
High in the hills, to lie there hand in hand
Like effigies and look up at the stars,
The never-setting ones set in the North
To circle the Pole in idiot majesty,
And wonder what was given them to wonder.

Being amateurs, they knew some of the names
By rote, and could attach the names to stars
And draw the lines invisible between
That humbled all the heavenly things to farm
And forest things and even kitchen things,
A bear, a wagon, a long-handled ladle;

Could wonder at the shadow of the world
That brought those lights to light, could wonder too
At the ancestral eyes and the dark mind
Behind them that had reached the length of light
To name the stars and draw the animals
And other stuff that dangled in the height,

Or was it in the deep? Did they look in
Or out, the lovers? till they grew bored
As even lovers will, and got up to go,
But drunken now, with staggering and dizziness
Because the spell of earth had moved them so,
Hallucinating that the heavens moved.

The End of the Opera

to Mona Van Duyn

Knowing that what he witnessed was only art,
He never wept while the show was going on.

But the curtain call could always make him cry.
When the cast came forward hand in hand
Bowing and smiling to the clatter of applause,
Tired, disheveled, sweating through the paint,
Radiant with our happiness and theirs,
Illuminati of the spot and flood,
Yet much the same as ordinary us.

The diva, the soubrette, the raisonneur,
The inadequate hero, the villain, his buffoon,
All equalled in the great reality
And living proof that life would follow life . . .

Though back of that display there'd always be,
He knew, money and envy, the career,
Tomorrow and tomorrow—it didn't seem
At that moment as if it mattered much
Compared with their happiness and ours
As we wept about the role, about the real,
And how their dissonances harmonized
As we applauded us: *ite, missa est.*

TRYING CONCLUSIONS

I

There is a punishment too smart for Hell,
And it is this: some people here on earth
Have been so hot at prayer that when they come
At last to bliss eternal they cannot stop
Blessing, beseeching, praising His Holy Name.

They would spend eternity hunkered on their knees
Without a cushion, save that the Infinite
Of wisdom and mercy pities them in the end.
They are the ones He will send to be born again.

II

What rational being, after seventy years,
When Scripture says he's running out of rope,
would want more of the only world he knows?

No rational being, he while he endures
Holds on to the inveterate infantile hope
That the road ends but as the runway does.

Acknowledgments

Many of the poems in "Trying Conclusions" first appeared in the following publications:

"Long Distance"—*Ploughshares*

"Magnitudes"—*Time*

"To the Congress of the United States, Entering Its Third Century"—*Congressional Record*, 3 March 1989

"The Process"—*St. Louis Post-Dispatch*

"Soundings"—*Southwest Review*

"Media"—*Mississippi Valley Review* and Pushcart Prize XVI selection, 1991

"Romantics" and "Answering Back"—*Lullwater Review*

"Analogies" and "Larkin"—*Prairie Schooner*

"The Evergreen"—*Ladies' Home Journal*

"Waste"—*PoetLore*

"A Keepsake for the Kids" and "The Amateurs of Heaven"—*The Formalist*

"August"—*Beloit Poetry Journal*

"The End of the Opera"—*The New Yorker*

"Trying Conclusions"—*The Laurel Review*

"Witnessing the Launch of the Shuttle Atlantis" was written for NASA; "Soundings" was written for the American Speech-Language-Hearing Association; "The Forbidden City" is published here courtesy of *Life Magazine;* and "Kicking Off the Combined Federal Campaign, October 11, 1988" was written for the occasion named.